CAPITAL
IS DEAD

CAPITAL
IS DEAD

MCKENZIE WARK

VERSO

London • New York

First published by Verso 2019
This paperback edition published by Verso 2021
© McKenzie Wark 2019, 2021

1 3 5 7 9 10 8 6 4 2

Verso

UK: 6 Meard Street, London W1F 0EG
US: 20 Jay Street, Suite 1010, Brooklyn, NY 11201
versobooks.com

Verso is the imprint of New Left Books

ISBN-13: 978-1-78873-533-9
ISBN-13: 978-1-78873-531-5 (UK EBK)
ISBN-13: 978-1-78873-532-2 (US EBK)

British Library Cataloguing in Publication Data
A catalogue record for this book is available from the British Library

The Library of Congress Has Cataloged the Hardback Edition As Follows:

Names: Wark, McKenzie, 1961- author.
Title: Capital is dead / McKenzie Wark.
Description: London ; New York : Verso, 2019. | Includes bibliographical
 references.
Identifiers: LCCN 2018059614| ISBN 9781788735308 (hardcover) | ISBN
 9781788735315 (United Kingdom ebook)
Subjects: LCSH: Capitalism.
Classification: LCC HB501 .W4395 2019 | DDC 332/.041—dc23
LC record available at https://lccn.loc.gov/2018059614

Typeset in Fournier by MJ & N Gavan, Truro, Cornwall
Printed and bound by CPI Group (UK) Ltd, Croydon, CR0 4YY

Contents

Introduction

> Post-capitalists' general strategy right now
> is to render language (all that which signifies)
> abstract therefore easily manipulable.
>
> —Kathy Acker

Which punk rock goddess are you? I'm Kim Gordon. Or I was. Not happy with that answer, I took the online quiz a few more times, until I got Patti Smith. I don't know what company made that quiz, but I agreed to give them access to a whole bunch of information in exchange for the privilege of playing it, in order to learn what I already know, that I'm more of a Patti Smith type than a Kim Gordon type.

The quiz held my attention for long enough to escape boredom, and it gave me something to post on social media, presumably to snag other people's attention. Some people get rather freaked out about algorithms that seem to know so much about us, although I always thought of privacy as a bourgeois concept.[1] What is dystopian here may be less the sharing of information than the asymmetry of the sharing.

If you are getting your media for free, this usually means that you are the product. If the information is not being sold to you, then it is you who are being sold. This is something that those of us in media studies have been teaching our students and telling the public since the broadcast era.[2] Back in the broadcast era, it was pretty simple. You listened to free radio or watched free television. In between the shows or the songs would be advertising. You were the product that was being sold, by the broadcaster, to advertisers. Or rather, what they sold was your *attention*.[3] In a time in which the quantity of information was rising and its cost plummeting, what was still rare and valuable was (and is) your attention.

In the broadcast era it was hard to even know whose attention a show gathered and whether any particular advertising worked. The ad industry guru David Ogilvy reported one of his clients claiming that half of his advertising worked and half of it failed, but he did not know which half was which.[4] A good deal of snake oil still goes into persuading ad buyers that advertisers have magical means of persuasion that will galvanize people's attention, lodge the brand in memory, and mobilize people's desire toward actually buying the product or—same thing really—voting for the candidate.

The evil genius of the postbroadcast-era media is that it not only holds our attention, it also records it. A lot more information can be extracted as to who we are, what we like, and which punk rock goddess we want to be. A lot of media consumers end up being quite shocked at just how much information about themselves they are giving away, and for free.[5] They had been gulled into treating postbroadcast media as if it were some sort of free public service, an illusion certain companies are quite happy to perpetuate to their users but certainly not to their investors. To their investors they tell a different story: that by giving away what looks like a free service, they can extract more information than they give and that they can monetize this asymmetry of information.[6]

The old culture industries had figured out how to commodify leisure.[7] The organized labor movement had struggled hard for free time for working people. Capital was forced to compromise, but it found a way to commodify leisure time as well as work time. The old culture industries at least had to make products that held our attention. In the postbroadcast era, the culture industries are superseded by the vulture industries. They don't even bother to provide any entertainment. We have to entertain each other, while they collect the rent, and they collect it on all social media time, public or private, work or leisure, and (if you keep your FitBit on) even when you sleep.[8] Which gives new meaning to a slogan invented by the Belgian surrealists: "Remember, you are sleeping for the boss!"[9]

Not just our labor, not just our leisure—something else is being commodified here: our sociability, our common and ordinary life together, what you might even call our communism.[10] Sure, it's not a utopian version of communism. It's a very banal and everyday one, it's our love of sharing our thoughts and feelings with each other and having connections to other people. But still, most people seem rather alarmed that their desire to share and be with each other, to reach out to friends, to pass on cat pictures, even their desire to have ferocious arguments with strangers, is making someone else very, very rich.

That people who use the Internet are tracked and monitored and turned into information is not even the half of it. If you think your social media is spying on you, just imagine what kind of information your bank has on you. There's a whole political economy that runs on asymmetries of information as a form of control.[11] It may even amount to a new kind of class relation. Sure, there is still a landlord class that owns the land under our feet and a capitalist class that owns the factories, but maybe now there's another kind of ruling class as well—one that owns neither of those things but instead owns the vector along which information is gathered and used.[12]

These days, not just everyone but everything is tracked and monitored and turned into information. If you order a package from an online website, you can follow the delivery of the item through its stages on its way to you. It's a consumer grade version of tracking the movement of everything: animal, mineral, and vegetable. For these purposes, even though you think you fall in the animal category, you are also being tracked as if you were a rock. The mineral sandwich in your pocket, your cellphone, is generating information about all of its movements.

Out of all of this information about the habits and movements of people and things, you can generate predictions about future movements. Well, *you* can't do that: while you produce this information, it all ends up privately owned by some information-centric company. You make the information, but like some kind of info-prole, you don't own the information you produce or the means of realizing its value. You don't get to benefit from its predictive power, although you will likely suffer the downside when those predictions prove spurious.

Because this vast, wonky information commons that we are all producing is privatized, it can be very hard to know how accurate or useful any of that information actually is.[13] Bullshit in = bullshit out. It becomes depressingly familiar to learn that algorithms have been primed with racist and sexist assumptions about the people it is supposed to neutrally observe.[14] This is annoying at the level of consumer profiling, but another thing entirely in the form of algorithmic policing.[15] However, it's a conversation frequently sidetracked into the demand for a fairer algorithm, as if there could still be a neutral third party above our differences, from which to pray for not much more than an equal right to be exploited by asymmetries of information. These discriminatory aspects of the information political economy need to be criticized and struggled over, but let's not lose sight of the bigger picture. That bigger picture is the information political economy as a whole.

Before focusing on what the corporations who own and control information are doing to us, let's pause to look at the peculiarities of the information itself.[16] Information is a rather strange thing. Contrary to the popular understanding, there's nothing ideal or immaterial about it.[17] Information only exists when there's a material substrate of matter and energy to store, transmit, and process it. Information is part of a material world. But it's a strange part. The word *information* is hardly new, but the science of information is very new; it is a postwar creation.[18]

Information is now such a pervasive organizing force that it has seeped into our worldview.[19] What we think of as "technology" these days very often means technologies that instrumentalize information. These are specific kinds of apparatus that gather, sort, manage, and process information so that it can then be used to control other things in the world. Information technology is a sort of meta-technology, designed to observe, measure, record, control, and predict what things, people, or indeed other information can or will or should do.

These technologies made information very, very cheap and very, very abundant. They gave rise to a strange kind of political economy, one based not only on a scarcity of things but also on an excess of information. This generated quite novel kinds of problems for those who had (or aspired to) power: how to maintain forms of class inequality, oppression, domination, and exploitation, based on something that in principle is now ridiculously abundant.

My proposition in this book is that resolving this contradiction called into being a new mode of production. This is not capitalism anymore; it is something worse. The dominant ruling class of our time no longer maintains its rule through the ownership of the means of production as capitalists do. Nor through the ownership of land as landlords do. The dominant ruling class of our time owns and controls information.

In other accounts, the strangeness of this state of affairs is elided by making it simply a variation on received ideas about Capital.[20] Just add a modifier to it: surveillance capitalism, platform capitalism, neoliberal capitalism, postfordist capitalism, and so on.[21] The essence stays the same, only the appearances change. But to sustain that argument, surely one has to at least entertain the thought experiment that this is no longer capitalism at all. Curiously, the attempt to make this thought experiment meets with strong resistance. Even critical theory seems very emotionally attached to the notion that capitalism still goes on, and on.

Against this trend, Paul Mason has risked the concept of postcapitalism, which has the merit of raising the stakes, even if it does not venture a language for an emerging mode of production. As Mason says, "The main contradiction today is between the possibility of free, abundant goods and information and a system of monopolies, banks and governments trying to keep things private, scarce and commercial."[22] Through a fresh reading of Marxist political economy, Mason offers a way of thinking how capitalism may have mutated that confounds received ideas about its form and trajectory. It's a stimulating read and implies two further projects: coming up with a renewed language for describing the present situation and identifying what in the received language about capitalism impedes forward movement in thought and action.

That this is not capitalism any more but something worse is a possibility I have tried out on all sorts of audiences, both activist and academic, for some years now. To some, this matches their experience and seems obvious, but it also meets with pretty strong resistance. There's a curious need to find reasons in advance not to think about it. Here might be the place to play postcapitalist bingo, where I list the most common reactions to even the possibility of thinking that this is no longer capitalism.

I am told that I am just talking about finance capitalism and that this is nothing new. (Sorry, but information has worked its way through the entire value production and reproduction cycle.) I am told I am just talking about circulation. (See previous answer.) I'm told that information is just ideas, which is idealism. Materialism is about matter. (Even the science of the mid-twentieth century had a more sophisticated "materialism" than that.)

I'm told that a lot of features of the present still look like the capitalism of the age of steam. (Yes, you can make it all look the same if you want, but let's try to focus also on what's not the same and account for both.) I'm told that since the telegraph existed in Marx's day, information is not all that new. (There are always historical precedents, long histories.) I'm told that to talk about information is the language of Silicon Valley. (Why let them monopolize the thinking about information as well as the actual information?)

I'm told (usually by some professor who has tenure) that Marx already explained everything in some obscure footnote in Volume 2 of *Capital* and that I should read the distinguished professor's very long exegesis of it. (Marx was not a professor, did not have tenure, and was trying to explain both continuity and change in his own historical time.) Or I am told, as if I did not know it, that the exploitation of labor still exists. (On that we can agree, but so does the extraction of rent from tenant farmers. Even slavery is not extinct. Modes of production co-exist and interact. I'm only asking if an additional one is emerging, not whether it describes the totality.)

Another objection is that I am only talking about the overdeveloped world, about Europe, Japan, and the United States. (Information is now the means to control global supply chains that reach deep into the so-called underdeveloped world.[23]) Or that I am only talking about the "tech" sector, which is not the same as the "real" economy. (This seems like an increasingly feeble objection, given how large the leading tech companies now are, measured by market capitalization.)

It is not just tech companies, however. As an example, let's look at a company that is hardly thought of as a tech sector marvel, but which happens to be the largest private employer in the United States: Walmart.[24] It's a company most would think of as a retailer. Walmart became famous both for selling very cheap consumer products and also for its ruthless exploitation of its workers and suppliers. On closer examination it is more of a logistics company, which succeeded also through using information to organize the flows of goods and labor through its distribution system. It was an early adopter among retailers of computerization. It even bought its own satellite to more efficiently manage its own data. Early on, founder Sam Walton found likely locations for stores by scouting from his own private plane, but this soon gave way to a "data-driven" approach.[25]

Walmart's infrastructure has a hub and spoke form, with box stores clustered around distribution centers. What is less well known is that it has almost as many data centers as physical distribution centers, and they are about as large. The parts that the consumer sees—the big box stores, the endless trucks on the road—are a physical expression of a computerized logistical system that determines where they will be and what they will do. It takes about as much infrastructure to organize the information as it does to organize the distribution of the physical stuff that ends up on the shelves, and with good reason: those data centers have to analyze all of the products and labor in motion and predict, out of every possible combination, what disposition of goods and labor should come next, and at every moment.

Those who shop there generate a fair amount of the information that drives the company. It is an asymmetrical exchange. You get a cheap pack of twelve toilet rolls. Walmart gets to add information about your actions into a predictive model that governs its business decisions. Those who work for Walmart are exploited labor. So too are those all the way down the supply chain to the factories and farms. And yet on top of that is something else: the extraction not just of physical labor from the bodies of workers, but the extraction of information from shoppers that Walmart does not even pay in exchange. It is this additional process—this information extraction process —that interests me. It turns out not to be unique to "tech," but rather an increasingly common "business model," and one not all that well described by classical models of capitalism. Maybe there are new forms of exploitation, inequality, and asymmetry as a layer on top of the old ones we're more used to.

Let's take a look at the second largest private employer in the United States: Amazon. It sells a product called Echo, which you put in your home somewhere so it can spy on you with its seven directional microphones. Some people are rather suspicious of this, but somehow the Amazon brand convinces many that this is okay. The Echo connects you to Alexa, an artificial intelligence whose objective is to learn your habits, needs, and desires—and service them. Over time it will get better at servicing you with information and products, and it will add what it learns from you to the matrix of what it knows about everybody. Your job, for which you are not getting paid, is to train a machine to know what the "human" is when seen entirely from the perspective of consuming.[26]

Echo and Alexa also hide from you everything that mediates between your enunciation of a desire and Amazon's fulfillment of it. Echo is the top layer of what Benjamin Bratton calls *the stack*.[27] Your desire has to be parsed into a form a machine can understand; that's the job of this *interface* layer.[28] The interface also positions you in relation to it, and to the rest of the stack, as a particular kind of subject: you are a user. Let's say you are a user who wants a book. You say: "Alexa, order me a copy of *Capital* by Karl Marx." Once you confirm that this is what you really want, this information will pass as if it were a vector, a particular kind of line, through a whole other series of layers of stack infrastructure, which will return this product to you, either immediately (if it is an e-book) or in a day or two (if it is a physical object). Each such expressed desire becomes a unique vector through a layered space that can fulfill an almost infinite number of desires, so long as they all take the form of a user asking an interface to satisfy a demand with a commodity. It does not really let you want or be much else.[29]

Your desire becomes a vector that will pass through many more layers of the stack. Bratton calls these the *address*, *city*, *cloud*, and *earth* layers. The *address* layer knows where you are, and it knows where the book that you want is, and it can calculate the optimal return vector to get one to the other to fulfill this desire. The *city* layer is where the physical part of the infrastructure resides. There is a warehouse, somewhere.[30] There is a server farm, somewhere; there are Amazon offices that design and manage and sell all this stuff—somewhere.

The *cloud* layer connects all these sites and many others together and performs the operations on the information gathered from all of them not only to fulfill orders and manage every vector, but also to learn from the aggregate of all of these actions and predict how else to extract information from them.[31] The *earth* layer is that from which the resources and energy to make and run this whole vast edifice to the digitized commodity are extracted.[32] Those resources are fed into sites of production that will make that book you ordered, or the t-shirt, or the sex toy, or whatever.

These sites of production too can be anywhere. A sophisticated logistics tracks and manages the flows of energy, labor, resources, and finished products through them.[33] The sites are usually where labor is cheap, exploitable, and held captive by borders and where there are few environmental regulations, but where there is a functional infrastructure of transport and shipping to move the resources and labor to the factory and the products out to some gated community nation in the overdeveloped part of the world where people get to order books or phones or Echos from Amazon. Container loads of those products sit, probably not for very long, in a warehouse where workers known as pickers dash about retrieving the products to meet the orders without even the time to stop for a toilet break, as all of their movements are tracked and measured in real time.[34]

Certainly, a lot of what just happened here could be called capitalism. Labor was corralled into factories and made to work long hours to make stuff. Other labor drove trucks or sat in call centers answering calls from irate users whose stuff did not arrive. But maybe there is something else here as well. Not just the exploitation of labor through the owning and controlling of the forces of production, but also the extraction of what you might call *surplus information*, out of individual workers and consumers, in order to build predictive models which further subordinate all activity to the same information political economy. One where you are nothing but a user, and everything you do within hearing range of Echo, or every movement you make with your cellphone, or everything you do on your laptop, or everything recorded of you or about you as you go about your daily life, is captured by a vector and fed into computation to figure out how better to use you for the greater glory of Amazon, Google, Apple or some other company, owned and controlled by a new kind of ruling class, the *vectoralist class*. To the vector the spoils.

Why is there so much resistance to even thinking about whether all this is a component of a new mode of production? I start in Chapter 1 with why we want to *believe* this is capitalism even if we hate it. If you take a step back, this really does seem a bit odd. Even its opponents have started to imagine that *Capital is eternal*. Perhaps it's time to ask whether the concept of Capital has ended up being rather more of a theological production than Marx would have intended. Hence *Capital is Dead* proceeds along two lines at once. It makes a minimally plausible case that the thesis of a new mode of production is worth investigating, and at the same time it is a critical account of how we got stuck trying to explain all emerging phenomena as if they were always expressions of the same eternal essence of Capital.

Most Marxists like to think they have separated themselves from religion but have made a religion of this separation.[35] If Capital is to function as a historical concept, then the question of how and when it ends has to be an open one. Where we seem to have ended up is with a not very logical but still emotionally compelling way of thinking: since communism has not prevailed, this must still be capitalism. The reality and the language of the present are anchored in an imaginary future. The challenge is to disenchant this myth of history without losing the ability to think of historical time as having other possibilities.[36]

Critical theories of the culture industry tend to stop short of thinking through the extent to which the production of critical theory itself is now a minor genre within the culture industry.[37] It has some of the characteristic hallmarks: a repetition of received ideas, narrative forms that resolve in predictable ways, a culture of exegesis that reproduces sameness. Critical theory becomes hypocritical theory. And so in Chapter 1, I try to combine the critical impetus of Marx with approaches to writing drawn from the historic avant-gardes that attempt to break from such habits, which treat writing as a more open-ended material practice.

Perhaps the writing of critical theory texts is part of the same information political economy as everything else. Perhaps the distinctive property form of the information commodity saturates such objects as it does so many other things. Perhaps treating the archive of such texts as the archive of private property is part of the problem. In Chapter 1, I advocate another relation to the archive, to writing, one advanced by the situationists: *détournment*. It works and plays as if writing were a practice of a literary communism.[38]

After looking at habits of belief and practices of writing, Chapter 2 elaborates on the thought experiment that this may not be capitalism any more, but something worse. Here I restate in condensed form an argument I first made in *A Hacker Manifesto* (2004), updated to take account of the further unfolding of the tendencies of this peculiar mode of production.[39] Here I assign its features some temporary names: I call the emerging ruling class the *vectoralist class*, because their class power derives from ownership and control of the vector of information.

The vector of information includes the capacity to transmit, store, and process information. It is the material means for assembling so-called big data and realizing its predictive potential. The vectoralist class owns and controls patents, which preserve monopolies on these technologies. It owns or controls the brands and celebrities that galvanize attention. It owns the logistics and supply chains that keep information in its proprietary stacks.

One thing that is distinctive about an information political economy is the way it instrumentalizes difference rather than sameness. The farmer and worker produce units of commodities that are equivalent within their kind. What I call the *hacker class* has to produce difference out of sameness. It has to make information that has enough novelty to be recognizable as intellectual property, a problem that landed property or commercial property does not have.

By hacker class I mean everyone who produces new information out of old information, and not just people who code for a living. Part of the struggle of our time is to see a common *class interest* in all kinds of information making, whether in the sciences, technology, media, culture, or art. What we all have in common is producing new information but not owning the means to realize its value. And yet the way we go about this is not quite the same thing as labor, just as being a worker is not quite the same thing as being a farmer. As is much clearer from Marx's political writings than from *Capital*, there are always many subordinate classes, just as there can be more than one ruling class.[40] Modes of production are multiple and overlapping.

Chapter 3 asks whether developments in the forces of production changed the relations of production and threw up a new kind of ruling class with different interests. But this is not a story where the forces of production are outside of historical struggle and simply develop on their own. On the contrary, the forces of production take a form determined by a series of class struggles as well. Who are the agents to that struggle? What role do scientists and engineers play? Could things have turned out otherwise?

To even ask this involves questions about the selective tradition within which we think about the twentieth century.[41] What we imagine happened, and who we imagine are the committed writers who struggled in and against it, is a picture mutilated by the Cold War.[42] The scientific left was stripped from the picture. They were Communists or fellow travelers. Their legacy has been suppressed, even on the left. Here I present the current state of the forces of production not as some supposedly inevitable outcome of the metaphysics of technics but as the result of a lost struggle over the form of technology and the labor of creating new information in scientific and technical fields.

The first time something like a transnational farmer, worker, and hacker alliance was even posited was in the thirties. It was subsumed into the global struggle against fascism and into Soviet realpolitik, and it was defeated (on both sides) by the Cold War. One of the consequences of defeat is the unchecked acceleration of more and more abstract forms of commodification, reaching from land to labor to information. The instrumentalization of information enables all of the earth to appear as a resource to be mobilized under the control of information, but where that control is based on information that treats everything, including information itself, as a commodity.

This might not be the commodity in its classical form, as Marx thought it in the middle of the nineteenth century.[43] The commodity form is not eternal. Commodification now means not the appearance of a world of things but the appearance of a world of *information about things*, including information about every possible future state of those things that can be extrapolated from a quantitative modeling of information extracted from the flux of the state of things, more or less in real time.[44] A commodity today appears as nothing but a vector, as a potential fulfilled through the interface of your phone or tablet or computer.

Looking closely at the forces of production is not quite the same thing as the study of technology. The difference is that the former asks questions about agency, and in particular class agency.[45] Chapter 4 brings us to a broader consideration of questions of class. Here, we look at what distinguishes Marxist approaches to class from other sociological theories. Once we have a means of analyzing class not just as a category but as forms of antagonism, we can ask whether new kinds of class relations may be emerging.

A class antagonism may arise out of relations of *property*, *authority*, or *expertise*.[46] If we combine thinking about emerging forces of production with attention to class, we can ask whether the production of information as a force of production also modifies class relations. The information vector is clearly connected to new kinds of property, authority, and expertise. While based in patent and copyright, intellectual property as a suite of near private property rights in all kinds of novel information is a relatively new development.[47] The evolution of these legal forms both responds to and further enables changes in the forces of production. Information also gave rise to new kinds of authority. We just don't live in Foucault's Panopticon. It's far worse. Whole new fields of expertise have emerged quite recently, reshaping the university and turning the university itself into a site for managing risk in the production of intellectual property.[48]

Chapter 4 is a slice through the social formation, showing its workings in cross section. Chapter 5 is a speculation on its genesis. It always seems strange to me that people who imagine they are thinking like Marxists offer a strictly idealist view of recent history: everything has changed because of ideas, and those ideas are "neoliberal." These then become policy and law through the agency of political actors.[49] This seems to me to betray every last principle of a materialist view of history. The irony is that in order to think a materialist history in a really quite "orthodox" way, one is forced to think in a heretical manner in relation to received ideas on the intellectual left.

The very same forces of production that enable this unprecedented mobilization of the world in the service of control through information also enable a science of the earth which shows conclusively that continuing to misvalue the whole of the world can't go on. Sooner or later (but probably sooner), it will crash the whole climate system of the planet.[50] Chapter 6 looks for ways to think about how the transformation of Capital beyond itself, into Vector, comes in contact with the very thing it lacks the means to properly know: the earth as the home from which it has expelled us.

There are two classic ways to think about capitalism being superseded by another mode of production. Either capitalism *accelerates* its movement to the point of qualitative transformation; or the proletariat that it produces as its own antagonist *negates* it from within.[51] The problem is that both of these are merely social theories, or at best, social-technical theories. Neither puts history back in the context of natural history, and in the era of the Anthropocene, of climate disruption and much else, that is the information that must be included in our thinking if it is to be at all timely.[52]

Chapter 6 adds two other kinds of historical narration into the mix. The first *extrapolates* from natural history, looking for ways we can learn about forms of organization of matter, energy, and information that are adaptable and enduring. Extrapolation is not reductionist, its key proposition is that very different kinds of form are possible at different scales of organization. Extrapolation opens the door to creative and speculative ways of producing collaborative knowledge across very different fields and assembling corresponding social movements. It's a way for the hacker class to think and act as a class, producing not only collaborative knowledge but also experimental prototypes of another way of life.

The counterpoint to this is what I call *inertia*. How is it that despite all the evidence that it is on a suicide mission, the current mode of production keeps accelerating toward failure? Why won't it change course? Where extrapolation stresses the possible connections between natural history and social history, inertia stresses the difference. We act in and against a world that remains other to us. Reduced to nothing but users, and our actions forced into the commodity form, our collective work and play produces a world over and against us, one that massively persists in its own habits of functioning.[53] Worse, collective human labor made a world for a ruling class that keeps making not only itself but us in its image.

Extrapolation opens exciting possibilities for thinking and acting collaboratively to build another civilization, here in the ruins of this one. Inertia is a sobering reminder of how hard that is going to be. I conclude *Capital is Dead* with a commentary on Raoul Peck's film *The Young Karl Marx* (2017). What I stress there is how Marx and his closest comrades changed the language and style of the progressive movements of their time. They freed themselves from received ideas, from selective tradition, even from radical selective tradition. In vulgar terms: they were punks.

Radicals can be the most conservative of people when it comes to *textology*, or faith in the exegesis of the written word from the archive as a form of knowledge.[54] We have to produce and defend knowledge in the face of a dominant ideology that insists that those texts are either useless or dangerous. (That it is an ideology is clear from its insistence in these incompatible faults). Wanting to move on from those cherished texts is assumed to be an attack on what they stood for. Sometimes the moment comes to summon your inner punk rock goddess and do things differently. Make some noise. Our knowledge-production methods might have become a bit too genteel for the times. It may at least be a better way to channel one's rage than ordering Patti Smith albums on Amazon.

Chapter 7 defends *vulgar Marxism* for its closeness to the everyday and to emerging technics of cultural and critical production. Here I look at four kinds of vulgar thinking, two from (or about) the twenties and two from the sixties. These are vulgarians who know something about how developments in the forces of production change the space of possibility for daily life and daily struggle. Unlike more genteel kinds of critical theory, they detect mutations in historical forms because they are not bound to residual and archaic forms of cultural work. They are already multiple and diverse, in terms of race, sex, sexuality, as the vulgar includes all of those excluded or marginalized within genteel institutions.

For years I was one of what the so-called alt-right calls a "cultural Marxist," interested mostly in what happens in the political and cultural superstructures of modern society, rather than in the technical and economic base. However, trying to understand culture will lead you to understanding media, which will lead you to try to figure out some things about technology. Then it turns out that the genteel forms of Western Marxist thinking taught in universities for several generations now are not good at understanding how the *forces of production* actually work.[55] That requires some actual technical knowledge and experience, or at least a willingness to concede that others may know about such things and to learn from them. The production of counterhegemonic knowledge can really only be comradely and collaborative.[56]

We have to start from the tensions apparent in the present and freely adapt the textual resources from the past to that situation. This might work better than starting with fidelity to the texts or events of the past and ignoring anything in the present that does not conform to them.[57] I read Peck's film as celebrating a will to transform even this closely cherished radical language in the interests of comprehending a present historical time in terms that enable it to appear as actionable, transformable. In that sense, it's a work of art that should give us courage to not just repeat the received ideas, even those of dear old Karl, but to embark on the collaborative production of a knowledge of the present that might help lead us out if it.

1

The Sublime Language of My Century

I wanted to speak
the beautiful language
of my century.

—Guy Debord

One thing that the left and right now seem to agree on is that the society in which we live is called *capitalism*.[1] And strangely enough, both now seem to agree that it is eternal. Even the left seems to think that there is an eternal essence to Capital and that only its appearances change. The parade of changing appearances yields a series of modifiers: this could be necro capitalism, communicative capitalism, cognitive capitalism, platform capitalism, neoliberal capitalism, or computational capitalism.[2] But short of an increasingly allegorical or messianic leap into something other, it is as if this self-same thing just went on forever.

I have a taste for the writerly tactics of modernism, so whenever I come across a piece of language about which there is such wide consensus I want to trouble it somehow.[3] This capitalism that we have all agreed that we live in, has it not become too familiar, too cozy, too roomy an idea? Why are we so *devoted* to its name? The reality the term tried to describe is, of course, far from comfortable. Capitalism is a world of exploitation, domination, and oppression. Capitalism, if this is what this still is, appears to be like a steam-hammer smashing not only the social but also the natural conditions of its existence to pieces. But then maybe this is the thing to ask about. Why have we become so comfortable with a way of describing an uncomfortable reality? Do we want a certainty in language that can't be had anywhere else?

That the world we live in is capitalism has become a familiar way of describing something that destroys what is familiar.[4] Capitalism atomizes and alienates. It renders everything precarious—except its own hold on the imagination. If the greatest trick of the devil was to persuade us that the devil does not exist, then maybe the greatest trick of capitalism is to gull us into imagining that there is nothing but eternal capitalism.

It is hard to describe things that change imperceptibly.[5] Some changes are like the crack in the china cup that just appears one day.[6] This may well be the level of language on which the problem rests. Language has to describe change using the combinations and permutations of terms that language offers: the *combinatory*. This combinatory of terms always has something of a binary quality.[7] If this is not capitalism, well then it must be communism, the term that negates it. Since this is obviously not communism, then it must still be capitalism after all. But what about when the change to be described doesn't correspond well to the neat digital chop between one term and another? Perhaps it is as hard to describe transitions between modes of production as it is to describe changes in mood.

There was once a language about transitions between modes of production. There's an elaborate argument about how feudalism became capitalism, about whether there might be multiple routes toward capitalism, about whether there could be more than one kind of socialism to come after. The debates about where capitalism came from are fascinating but mostly of academic interest.[8] The debates about where it might go got caught up in Cold War discourse; with the demise of the Soviet Union, they appear to be moot. With the truncating of the historical time line to the chunk in the middle called capitalism, the historical imagination finds itself reduced as well.

That language tends to work this way leaves us with a very odd situation. Now, both the left and the right alike end up working within the same language about this being capitalism. It was surely not Marx's intention that the language he brought together to get critical leverage on his times would become commonplace terms also used by our enemies. Among other qualities as a writer, Marx really was one of the great modern poets.[9] He made modifications to the language that have stuck. Of course he worked with the materials of the languages he had at hand, but he wrought something lasting: a combinatory of terms, a matrix of concepts, for describing History.[10] Like any great poetic corpus, his work contains multitudes. But a few standard permutations came to stick in the mind, like great pop songs, although maybe with misremembered lyrics.[11]

Here I think is his greatest hit, his epic track, the one that has become something of an earworm. Here's how it goes: this is capitalism. It has an essence and it has appearances. Its appearances are false, a phantasmagoria of fetishes, in which commodities appear as if endowed with self-moving spirit. Its real essence is defined by these things: the commodity form, with its doublet of use value and exchange value; by labor's double form, as concrete labor and abstract labor; by the extraction of surplus value in the production process, by the wage relation, by the rising organic composition of capital, in which more and more of it is made up of dead labor rather than living labor, by the crisis caused of the tendency of the rate of profit to fall. And finally, by negation.[12]

One could debate endlessly whether this is what Marx really meant, but I think that's a fair condensation of how many have heard him. It's a sort of ur-version of Marx that has become something of a refrain. Or even a myth. There are actually two main variants of the myth here about negation. Either capitalism negates itself, brought to ruin by its own contradictions. Or it is negated by a subject that it produces as its own negation, the working class. In either variant, one thing is key: until the moment of negation, capitalism can change its appearances but never its essence. Its essence can only be negated by contradiction or struggle. Assorted variant tunes spill out of this rhetorical frame, mutating like genres of techno music.

There are other ways to perform variations on Marx's combinatory of terms. For instance, one can swap out the abstract verb *negation* and replace it with *acceleration*. This approach was popular again in the early twenty-first century, as it was in the early twentieth century.[13] Here the idea is that there's nothing that can negate capital, either in its own contradictions or in the force it produces in and against itself. Rather, the best one can do is accelerate it to its end, toward a Promethean leap into another mode of production.[14] But note that this is not as much a change in tune as its advocates like to imagine. It leaves intact the mythic form of Capital as an essence.

Yet faith in either the negation or acceleration of Capital has grown faint. The essence of Capital is eternal—this is the striking feature of how it is now imagined.[15] Naturally, those who love it embrace this thought. It needs merely to be perfected by our love. This is sometimes called (with a stunning lack of imagination) *neoliberalism*. But what is even stranger is that those who do not love it seem to agree.[16] The essence of Capital is eternal. It goes on forever, and everything is an expression of its essence. Capital is the essence expressed everywhere, and its expression is tending to become ever more total.

The other side of the eternal essence of Capital is its ever-changing appearances. Change is accounted for through the use of modifiers. Its appearances can even be periodized. There was merchant capitalism, then liberal capitalism, then monopoly capitalism, then neoliberal capitalism. (Let's not even mention that other and more problematic category, the Asiatic mode of production, because that was not supposed to have a history.[17])

There's some ambiguity as to what to call the current stage, however. It could be *disaster*, *cognitive*, *semio*, *neuro*, *late*, *biopolitical*, *neoliberal*, or *postfordist capitalism*, to name just a few options.[18] Note that the last two are temporal modifications to a modifier: *neo*liberal, *post*fordist. Could there be any better tribute to the complete enervation of the imaginal faculty by capitalism, or whatever it is, that this is the best our poets can do?[19] Modify the modifier?

Besides adding modified modifiers to the sacred category of Capital, another variant is worth a mention, one that works on different terms within the combinatory. This is a poetics that opens a split within its essential categories. Its partisans tend to go a bit overboard with the binary difference between two terms that emerges out of the split, although they have not been so bold as to break too much with the essence of capitalism. Rather, it worked like this: there used to be *material* labor; now there is *immaterial* labor. It's a different kind of labor. It's the opposite! But what this labor produces, and is exploited by, is still only a modified capitalism, a *cognitive* capitalism.[20] It's not material any more. Capitalism itself is about ideas.

It's striking how much one can get carried away with the play of language and forget to look at the world. Somehow, I don't think the tens of millions of industrial workers in China perceive their work as immaterial.[21] Nor does this strange immaterial labor of the overdeveloped world happen without an extensive technical apparatus, indeed a whole new suite of forces of production, a stack of vectors, an infrastructure—call it what you like.

The task of this little book is thus a provocation: to think the possibility that capitalism has already been rendered historical but that the period that replaces it is worse. That it could be worse gets us away from the happy narratives in which latter-day capitalism is the magic kingdom, free from contradiction and class struggle, where History ends.[22] Rather, in this thought experiment, I propose to write the present as including a new kind of class conflict, including new kinds of class, arising out of recent mutations in the forces and relations of production. By putting this pressure on our received ideas and legacy language, perhaps we can begin to see the outlines of the present afresh, estranged from our habits of thought.

There was once a grand attempt to have done with at least part of this great epic-poetic edifice. It started with questioning the idea of Capital as having an essence and an appearance. What if appearances were as real as the essence? Before addressing that, let's add just a little more nuance. There were actually two versions of the essence–appearance structure. One took the economic to be the essence, but in the sense of being the base, and everything else is built upon on it. This rather vulgar version is called *economism*. In the other version, it's not the economic, but the commodity form that is the essence, one that has come into being in history and then become the essence of history, which records its forms of appearance as a false totality or as spectacle.[23]

Against this, Louis Althusser took the view that the economic base only determined everything else in the last instance. The political and cultural superstructures were not mere appearances. They have their own material form, but one whose function is the reproduction of the essential economic form of capitalism.[24] Whatever its merits, this version was like catnip to academic Marxists looking for ways to fit into conventional academic disciplines, because it allowed for three distinct objects of study: the economic, the political, and the ideological (or cultural). These conceptual objects conveniently correspond to those of existing academic disciplines.

If things like politics or culture are relatively autonomous super-structures of an economic base, and if they have their own material form, maybe they even have their own essence! It did not take long for culture to have its own essential categories, borrowed from linguistics: the signifier and the signified were just like exchange value and use value. An abstract essence! A *different* one! So one could just specialize in singing the song of this (relatively) autonomous world of essences and appearances, while still gesturing to the master narrative, that this is indeed and will remain capitalism.[25]

If the economy has an essence and appearances, and culture has an essence and appearances, then maybe politics does too. The wonderful thing about language is that if you seek it, you can find it. Yes, politics has an essence too! It is The Political, the great fundamental drama of friend versus enemy, or maybe it's dissensus, or something.[26] The main thing is that we can sing the song of the essence and appearances of politics, while still gesturing to the master narrative, that this is indeed and will remain capitalism.

I have to say that my inner modernist finds this all rather banal. Is this the best we can do to speak the sublime language of our century?[27] Why does it all seem the same, like pop music? Variations on themes, all leading back to the same old note, that capital is eternal? One day (that never comes) there will be a messianic leap into something else.[28] It seems to me that our poetry of capitalism, or whatever this is, shows all the signs of being a culture industry. Nowhere in these tunes is there that striking note of nonequivalence or that moment of defamiliarization when the roof falls in.[29]

One has to ask: what is the emotional attachment that we have to the idea that this is capitalism and that it is eternal?[30] It has to be said that the most vigorous attempts to tell a different story, to strike a different tune, were made in bad faith. There was a time when it was a popular art form. While the Soviet Union claimed ownership of the narrative of capitalism and its coming negation, you could make a good living in the "free world" coming up with a different story. Not surprisingly, it was former Marxists and socialists who wrote most of those alternative epic poems that sprouted into whole worldviews.

These former Marxists would sing of the glories of the "managerial revolution," of the "postindustrial society," of the conditions for "take-off" and growth, of the "future shock" of technological disruption. What these epic narratives all had in common was that they accepted the basic Marxist combinatory of terms for understanding History. They conceded its power, its poetry.[31]

But they changed the ending. Rather than negation, the story ends with Capital resolving its own contradictions. It's a happy ending that Theodor Adorno would have called an *extorted reconciliation*.[32] This mytho-poetics had some currency during the Cold War. But with the collapse of the supposedly socialist world of the Soviet Union, which claimed all subsidiary rights to the great Marxist story, these counternarratives lost their force.

One influential counterstory from the twentieth century survives. The author who inspired it, Joseph Schumpeter, was not a socialist, although he briefly worked for a socialist government.[33] He probably got it from that original Marxist sellout, Werner Sombart. In this play on the combinatory of Marxist language, Capital affirms itself continually by negating itself continually. It negates itself, and in an affirmative way, as "creative destruction." It can "disrupt" itself! Indeed, its essence becomes its self-disruption. And it is our sacred duty never to get in its way. In our own times this old story was adapted into the belief system of the so-called tech industry, as a part of what Richard Barbrook calls the *California Ideology*.[34] Into it can be folded certain other variations, about the "fourth industrial revolution," for example.[35]

The conceit of all these postcapitalist stories was that this is not the same old capitalism—it's better! When people hear the beginnings of a story about this no longer being capitalism, their resistance generally rises. Unless you happen to be worth several million dollars, the chances are you do not perceive this as something better than capitalism or a capitalism that always improves on itself.

Maybe it would be interesting, aesthetically and politically, to take the other fork of possible epic-poetic combinations of terms. Instead of the line that this is not capitalism, it's better, what if we explored the line that this is not capitalism, but worse? This meets a lot of resistance too. This I can tell you from experience, having tried to write variations on this text for fifteen years.[36] Nobody wants to leave the certainty of the devil they know, or think they know, for something that promises to be worse.

So the bad news is: this is not capitalism anymore, it's something worse. And the good news is: Capital is not eternal, and even if this mode of production is worse, it is not forever. There could be others. That's the struggle today. OK, so that's not particularly good news. But there is also this: an end to left-melancholia, that eternal sadness about eternal capitalism.[37]

Interestingly, few people will even attempt to think Capital-is-dead even as a thought experiment. There really is something fundamental to the myth that this is capitalism, as if Capital were the name of a God. It may even be the defining feature of ideology today. Ideology today is not the acceptance of a neoliberal *structure of feeling* or habits of thought and action.[38] Ideology today is clinging to the belief that this is capitalism. To think that we live in an illusory world of *capitalist realism* still might concede too much reality to the belief in eternal Capital.[39]

I think it's time to be bold. Let's reanimate Marx's infamous remark: "All I know is that I am not a Marxist."⁴⁰ What if we took that in the sense that he was not one of those who simply took a language and a poetic form extracted from his predecessors as a given? He was, to the contrary, the one who had constructed that language with a quite particular purpose in mind: to understand the situation of his times *from the labor point of view*. So: what if we kept the commitment to understanding, not his situation, but ours, from the labor point of view—whatever that might mean now—and bracketed off the rest?

That makes a certain sense to me. I really am puzzled by why we should use blocks of linguistic material from his time to understand our time. Why use Marx's playful modifications of the fashionable philosophy, the popular science, the political tracts, or the technological metaphors of the mid-nineteenth century? When poets or novelists inhabit old forms like that, we immediately think it's dated or ironically retro. But somehow we want our critical theory to still be about eternal Capital, as if it were some subgenre of steampunk.⁴¹

Different genres of text have a different relationship to tradition and innovation, and at different moments in their development. They aren't always in synch. There's generally a culture industry that pulps the more innovative texts into sameness and an avant-garde trying to escape that sameness and do something else. If you are trying to write an interesting (rather than merely successful) novel or poem, you want to change things at the formal level, rather than ship your wine in the same old bottles. The thing is, where readings and rewritings of Marx are concerned, they seem to me to belong to the culture industry. It's a commonplace now to read *Capital* as a work of philosophy or even as a novel, but to do so with a distinctly un-Marxist reverence.⁴²

Like everything else, the transmission of the Marxian corpus through time is a matter of what Raymond Williams called *selective tradition*.⁴³ Most textology of Marx deploys conventional protocols of *quotation, exegesis,* and *interpretation.*[44] In these habitual readings, selections from the canonic texts are made to yield an underlying meaning that subtends them. The texts count as evidence that represents an underlying essence.

Where Capital is thought as an essence that produces appearances that are false, the Marx-corpus is read as an appearance that is true to an essence—most of the time. Marx's texts can be discreetly corrected to correspond to their true essence. (Writing this sort of Marx fan-fiction gives our conservative textologists enough of a thrill of originality). This essence is the veracity against which the false appearances of the world are then held to account.

Alternatively, rather than read the Marx-corpus through the interpretive filter of a Marx essence, Marx texts can be read through the interpretive filter of someone else's text. This yields all of the *supplemental Marxisms:* Marx read through structuralism, psychoanalysis, deconstruction, and so on.[45] Rather than a Marx-corpus read in terms of its fidelity to a Marx-essence that it resembles, this procedure is a bit different. It yields a Marx who says something other than what he probably thought he meant to say. There's still a "real" Marx, to be interpreted, but it may be at variance with the surface of the text. Capitalism can then be read in terms of what this other Marx meant, and the surface effects of Marx that don't conform to it are themselves residues of Capital itself.

Pursued to its limit, this method tends to become post-Marxist, when Marx himself appears to be more symptom than diagnosis.[46] One ends up saying, with Foucault: "Marxism exists in the nineteenth century like a fish in water: that is, unable to breathe anywhere else."[47] The paradox here is that because the reading protocols operating in the selective tradition of Marxism are rather conservative, Marx ends up snagged on the language of his times. His combinatory is not really opened up to play freely in our times.

All of this takes as a given the transmission of Marx common to non-Marxist and even post-Marxist philosophers and other humanities or social science scholars and the not very different approach of rather scholastic party functionaries of Marxism's "classical" period.[48] There are other readers of Marx, and some of them are poets, or who read as poets do. Modern poets, less interested in the meaning of the texts (the always deferred *signified*) than in the signs themselves (the materiality of the *signifier*).[49] One that has been of particular use to me is something that is much less a method of reading and more a procedure for writing: what Guy Debord called *détournement*.[50] The word includes the sense of the detour, the turning aside, a hijacking but also a seduction.

Debord: "The device of *détournement* restores all their subversive qualities to past critical judgments that have congealed into respectable truths ... The defining characteristic of this use of *détournement* is the necessity for distance to be maintained toward whatever has been turned into an official verity ... Ideas improve. The meaning of words has a part in this improvement. Plagiarism is necessary, progress implies it. Staying close to an author's phrasing, plagiarism exploits his expressions, erases false ideas, replaces them with correct ideas ... *Détournement* is the antithesis of quotation, of a theoretical authority invariably tainted if only because it has become quotable, because it is now a fragment torn away from its context, from its own movement ... *Détournement* is, by contrast, the fluid language of anti-ideology ... Détournement founds its cause on nothing but its own truth as critique at work in the present."[51]

Debord's writing itself is a brilliant *détournement* of Marx and Lautréamont (and much else), one that generated a style (and some fresh concepts) for understanding the historical moment of the mid-twentieth century. Marx: "The wealth of those societies in which the capitalist mode of production prevails, presents itself as an immense accumulation of commodities ..." Debord: "The whole life of those societies in which modern conditions of production prevail presents itself as an immense accumulation of spectacles."[52]

And so, once more, comrades, if we would become critics of our times! Let's try some more *détournement* to produce some different language out of that which comes down to us, rather than trying to interpret the eternal essence of the text as if we could reproduce it as more of the same. To practice the style of negation today requires the negation of some old styles.

But how do we broach the question of style in Marx? For Keston Sutherland *Capital* needs readers rather than "curators of concepts."[53] *Capital* is written in clashing styles, aimed at a readership Marx knew to be divided by class. To the bourgeois reader, aping genteel sensibilities, Marx addresses himself as a satirist, writing at the expense of the myths the bourgeois lives by. For instance, Sutherland claims that Marx's famous overture on the fetish character of the commodities has been "influentially mistranslated" in accounts that try to master the text by extracting its concepts.[54]

Commodity fetishism is not a misapprehension of the commodity.[55] Marx is saying something about the making of the commodity itself. Human labor is not just abstracted into a homogenous quantity in the commodity form. Labor gets minced and boiled into *Gallerte*: aspic, meat jelly. Or in today's terms into something like what appears in those truly disgusting online videos that show the extrusion from some machine of that major ingredient of hamburgers: *pink goo*.

Sutherland: "The living hands, muscles and nerves of the wage laborer are mere 'animal substances,' ingredients for the feast of the capitalist."[56] Marx's image of what happens to labor is not a genteel conceptual abstraction but a vulgar image from industrial butchery. "The object of Marx's satire on abstract human labor is not the worker

33

reduced to a condiment but the bourgeois consumer who eats him for breakfast."[57]

Capital is "a work of sustained, aggressively satirical détournement in which the risks and failures of style are arguments in themselves, irreducible to theoretical proposition."[58] Elsewhere, Marx détourns phrases from Dante, Goethe, and Shakespeare, erasing false ideas, replacing them with correct ones. The fetish character of commodities is a *détournement* of a work of racist ethnography by Charles De Brosse.[59]

In the De Brosse source text, the genteel and enlightened reader is first astonished that stupid "savages" worship fetishes, but disciplines this astonishment into knowledge. In Marx it is the reverse. The commodity appears at first as something rational and known to the genteel sensibility, but on closer inspection is quite astonishing. It is we, gentle reader, who are stupid before the fetish. There is no reconciliation to this strange thing. It has to be abolished.

To write after Marx is not to claim a genteel mastery of concepts alone. Where I would press on (which Sutherland very likely wouldn't) is to suggest that one way to restore a certain vulgar energy to writing might be to take Marx's tactics of *détournement* and apply them to the concepts of eternal Capital that have been extracted from *Capital* itself in certain genteel readings and perpetuated as a kind of myth.

The truth of the matter is that Marxist writing itself became ideological. Its acquiescence to the sense of capitalism being eternal is one sure sign of this. Hence the necessity of the gesture, the thought experiment, of declaring: *Capital is dead*. It is dead like God before it, and as with that discovery, to announce this is treated in the "marketplace of ideas" as madness. The corpus of Marx is read within a textology of transmission, using scholastic protocols of quotation, exegesis, and interpretation descended from those developed for religious texts.[60] And so not surprisingly Marxism became a minor form of (protestant!) religion—one of the boring ones, with long sermons and much commentary on scripture.

To interrupt these habits requires not another reading of Marx, promising to peel away the false and reveal the true essence. Rather, it takes another style of writing. *Détournement* does not care about the self-identity of the textual corpus or the eternal spirit hidden within. It takes what it finds useful or amusing for composing the textual expression of the present situation. Judged in relation to the sacred scriptures it will of course appear as heretical, mad, wrong, or vulgar. This is a poetics that *intends* to differ from the material it appropriates.

Détournement is no respecter of private property or public propriety. It has no interest in those who claim Marx (or for that matter Debord) as their patrimony, as the field they alone are warranted or patented to cultivate and trade. Our task, in the thought experiments gathered here, is to appropriate from the Marxist tradition for the composition of frankly Frankensteinian monster-texts whose only interest is in being anti-ideological tactics, in pointing from within the combinatory of terms to the limits of what Flaubert called *received ideas*.[61] There's not much choice but to work with received ideas, but there's more than one way to select from tradition.

So let's think about the present on these terms: what if, rather than start at the beginning, one started at the end? The capitalism story always starts in the past, with the birth of capitalism, and imagines a destiny, a teleology, wherein the present must be some continuum from that past.[62] This must be some modification of the essence of the thing. Let's do it the other way around. Let's first describe the present, then secondarily figure out where it came from. This may even, in the end, involve modifying our understanding of capitalism's pasts.

Any attempt to describe the present in its own language is more than likely to end up reproducing the language of its ruling class at best, or at worst the left-over language of obsolete ruling classes. Hence the method of *détournement*, appropriating received ideas, but also erasing and correcting. Let's pick a Marx text to *détourn*. Rather than start where Marx more or less ended, with *Capital*, let's start where his "mature" work began, with the Preface to the *Contribution to the Critique of Political Economy*.[63] Let's start not with capitalism, as if we could just assume that is what this still is. Let's start with Marx's sketch of how to think about *modes of production*. I have only modified it slightly.

In the social-technical production of their existence, humans inevitably enter into definite relations, which are independent of their desires, namely relations of production appropriate to a given stage in the development of their material forces of production (and reproduction). The totality of these relations of production constitutes the economic structure of society, the infrastructure, on which arises a legal, political and cultural superstructure. The mode of production of material life conditions the general process of social, political, and cultural life. It is not the ideologies of humans that determine their social-technical existence, but their social-technical existence that determines their ideologies.

Accidents happen in the course of historical development. The forces of production come into conflict with the existing relations of production or—this just says the same thing in legal terms—with the property relations within the framework of which they have operated hitherto. From forms for the development of the productive forces, these relations turn into their fetters. Then begins an era of transformation of the superstructures. The changes in the forms of social-technical metabolism lead sooner or later to the transformation of the whole immense superstructure.

In studying such transformations, it is always hard to distinguish between the material transformation of the conditions of production, which can be determined with the methods of a social science, and the legal, political, religious, artistic, or philosophic—in short, the mythic or ideological forms in which humans sense and feel this conflict and fight it out. Just as one does not judge an individual by a Facebook profile, so one cannot judge such a period of transformation by its myths.

On the contrary, these myths must be explained from the contradictions of material life, from the conflict existing between the social-technical forces of production and the relations of production. No social order is ever destroyed before all the productive forces for which it is sufficient have been developed, and more abstract relations of production never replace older ones before the material conditions for their existence have matured within the framework of the old society.

Social-technical forms of organization thus usually set themselves only such tasks as they are able to solve, since closer examination will always show that the problem itself arises only when the material conditions for its solution are already present or at least in the course of formation. In broad outline, the ancient, feudal, despotic, capitalist, and *vectoralist* modes of production may be designated as epochs marking the extension of the exploitation of nature by social-technical forms of increasing abstraction. The capitalist mode of production was imagined to be the last antagonistic form of the social process of production. Marx thought that "the prehistory of human society accordingly closes with this social formation."[64] On that, he was mistaken.

2

Capitalism—or Worse?

Inside the factory, you are endlessly doing.
You are inside, in the factory, the universe,
the one that breathes for you.

—Leslie Kaplan

To be working, as vernacular English has it, is to be on your *grind*; work, says Marx, is a meat grinder. Wage labor ends up reduced to blood and guts and goo, minced and reduced to aspic, to dead flesh to be slurped down by a capitalist ruling class. It's a suitably vulgar image. Capital appears as something monstrous, as a vampire living on the blood of others. Let's be a bit careful with making monsters appear as the bad guy, however.[1] The moral force of assigning the role of monster to the other has a lot of valences.

There's another problem with this line of satirical style: it may describe a lot of what wage labor is like in the world, but it is also possible that *you*, dear reader, spend your working hours sitting in front of a laptop or taking meetings. There's a world of everyday life the meat grinder doesn't describe from which a surplus is extracted for another's benefit in other ways.[2] You can be someone other than a tenant farmer or an industrial worker and still not be a capitalist or even petit bourgeois.

There's a whole other repertoire of popular images that address this experience, at least in part. In the Wachowski sisters' movie, *The Matrix*, it's the scene where Neo, the protagonist, is rescued.[3] It turns out he is not living the life of a hacker that he thinks he is. Rather, he inhabits a pod full of goo, in a vast array of such units, with a giant plug in the back of his skull sucking energy from his gray matter for some unseen ruling power. He glimpses a sublime landscape of endless rows of such pods for just a moment before he is whisked away.

A less successful but even more creepy version is the TV show Joss Whedon created with Eliza Dushku, *Dollhouse*.[4] The Dollhouse is a clandestine business that rents out bodies to powerful people. These bodies can be programmed with the emotional range and intellectual talents of other humans. Often they are sexy spies or performers of subtle kinds of emotional labor.[5] Upon return from their missions, their brains are "wiped" and they loll about in a fugue state, taking yoga classes, practicing "wellness," and eating from the organic buffet. They were lured into this line of work with contracts that promise they will return to their real selves with no memory and a bunch of money, but often they are relegated to the Attic, where it turns out their brains are used as meat-ware nodes of the computer that runs the whole thing.

One version of these anxious, creepy stories about this odd kind of not-quite-labor today has the emotional and cognitive capacities of the human reprogrammed and used by a ruling power. Another version reverses the combinatory elements. The human body is used as a vehicle and has its cognition erased, used instead by a ruling power. In Jordan Peele's *Get Out*, the takeover is racialized.[6] Powerful white people implant their own brains in Black skulls. In Anne

Leckie's science fiction novel *Ancillary Justice*, the bodies of enslaved peoples become ancillaries to the great artificial intelligence-driven military spaceships of an intergalactic empire, whose ruling culture is a kind of liberal imperialist feminism that suggests Hillary Clinton.[7]

The Cuban science fiction writer Agustín de Rojas offers a rather more complex take on the same mythic material. In *The Year 200*, communism has more or less triumphed, but it has not pursued a truly radical integration of the human into inhuman information technology.[8] Agents of the defeated Empire of Capital freeze and miniaturize themselves, lie dormant underground awaiting a more complacent stage in communist development, and then return to the surface and start taking over the bodies of the comrades. All that stands against the Empire is one of their own, who is actually a Communist double agent. She takes as her ally a cyborg-woman who is no longer quite of our species. Both the communist good guys and capitalist bad guys are "monstrous" inhumans in this story, but there's more than one way to be other than human.

Industrial capitalism was not terribly interested in workers who think and feel. It wanted hands. It wanted muscle. It was a flesh-eating machine. Whatever disgusting and terrifying power lurks in these more recent stories does not so much eat bodies as brains. This combinatory works two ways: either your mind is erased and your body is another mind's vehicle; or your mind is subordinated to the will of another power.[9] Either way, your mind is not your own. It feels like some vile takeover. But what if this isn't just a takeover, but a whole new class relation?

Let's start thinking through this curious class relation by being very "orthodox." Let's start with the *forces of production*, the *relations of production* that correspond to them, the class antagonism generated out of those relations of production, and the political and culture *superstructures* that correspond to that base.[10] And let us also try to describe, just as Marx did, what may be emerging rather than what is established. If one starts with what is established, it is easy to interpret any new aspect of the situation as simply variations on the same essence. Starting with what may be emerging provides a suitable derangement of the senses, a giddy hint that all that was solid is melting into air.[11]

The thought experiment that might result is quite simple. Here's a sketch, to be elaborated upon as we go: There really is something qualitatively distinct about the forces of production that eat brains, that produce and instrumentalize and control information. This is because information really does turn out to have strange ontological properties. Making information a force of production produces something of a conundrum within the commodity form. Information wants to be free but is everywhere in chains.[12] Information is no longer scarce, it is infinitely replicable, cheap to store, cheap to transmit, and yet the whole premise of the commodity is its scarcity.

Information as a force of production calls into being particular *relations* of production and is at the same time formed by those relations. In classic Marxist style, one can look here at the evolution of legal forms.[13] In the late twentieth century "intellectual property" emerged as almost an absolute private property right.[14] One that makes the once separate and local property forms of patent, copyright, and trademark equivalent and exchangeable forms of private property. These forms need transnational legal enforcement, precisely because information is such a slippery and abstract thing.[15]

And so, like the enclosures or the joint-stock company before it, intellectual property law becomes the form of a new kind of relation of production, more abstract than its predecessors, and one that makes not land or physical plant, but rather information itself, a form of private property. Like those preceding forms of private property, this one crystalizes into a class relation. As an absolute form of private property, it creates classes of owners and nonowners of the means of realizing its value. Land as private property gave rise to the two great classes of *farmer* and *landlord*. Capital as private property gave rise to the two great classes of *worker* and *capitalist*. Is there a new class relation that emerges out of the commodification of information?

For this thought experiment, let's say it does. I call those classes the *hacker class* and the *vectoralist class*. The hacker class produces new information. But what is "new" information? It is whatever intellectual property law recognizes as new. It's a strange kind of production. Where the farmer grows crops through a seasonal cycle and the worker stamps out repetitive units of commodities, the hacker has to use their time in a different way, to turn the same old information into new. Getting this done is not like the seasonal repetitions of farming or the clocking-on of the worker. It happens when it happens, including time spent napping or pulling all-nighters.[16] The workplace nightmare of the worker is having to make the same thing, over and over, against the pressure of the clock; the workplace nightmare of the hacker is to produce *different* things, over and over, against the pressure of the clock.

The characters of Peggy and Don in the TV series *Mad Men* work as midcentury prototypes.[17] It's the advertising business during the golden years of Fordism.[18] Don is a creative, struggling within the agency with its owners to become an owner too. Peggy is a secretary, a white collar worker, and her struggle is to become a creative. Meanwhile, Joan is already at the top of the secretarial pool, managing it, but wants to become an owner. As the show progresses, the women make a little headway in this male business. By show's end, Black women are just starting to get the secretarial jobs, but the computer has arrived and will make some of them obsolete anyway. Like much of bourgeois culture, it is a small business narrative, which compresses the classes and blurs the lines between them. The prize of becoming truly ruling class is always just out of reach.

For our purposes, the interesting part is its picture of the activities of one prototype of the hacker class. The camera is fascinated by Don and Peggy actually doing their jobs. Don takes long naps on his office sofa. Sometimes he just wanders off. The material for his brilliant ad campaigns come from all sorts of incidental sources. He drinks too much, tries smoking pot. The whole office takes amphetamine shots and pulls an all-nighter, making speed-induced creative work full of tremendous energy and really bad decisions. Meanwhile Peggy manages to transition from worker to hacker because she actually knows something about how to address the desires of women, but she ends up limited and stymied in all sorts of ways by an industry that does not know the value of her difference.

The less popular series *Halt and Catch Fire* shows us the early tech industry version of the same set of activities, this same work that isn't quite regular work.[19] Hackers can't be managed like farmers or workers; they are not the same as either class. There's no relation between the units of labor time and the units of value produced. Something cooked up on the spur of the moment might have enormous value. Long hours of slog might end up being for nothing. Being exempt from routine work is not really all that glamorous in either story, as it just brings uncertainty, frustration, pressure, and (for some) madness.

Both of these shows hinge on the desire to escape from the limits of the hacker class and become owners. That's the limit to the desire the culture industry can admit for this class. And yet both these shows portray a continual treadmill of hope and failure. Like the farmer and the worker, the hacker does not usually end up owning the product of her efforts. Unless you own a drug company or a tech company or media conglomerate, you have to sell the rights to what you produce.

It is not always the same as selling labor power. You might still own the intellectual property, for example. But the hacker rarely captures much of the value of what they create or invent.

Nobody else gets to be Google's Sergey Brin precisely because there is a Sergey Brin, who is not the avatar of the hacker class, but of its opposite—the *vectoralist class*. He is the real unicorn: the hacker become owner. The one that perpetuates the myth that drives a million start-ups on the path to the same desire, not realizing that it is the very thing that now blocks that desire. It is highly unlikely that your start-up will be the next Google. At best, you might sell it to Google or to some other avatar of the vectoralist class.

The vectoralist class owns and controls the *vector*, a concept I use to describe in the abstract the infrastructure on which information is routed, whether through time or space.[20] A vector in geometry is simply a line of fixed length but of unfixed position. It's a way of thinking about a technology as having something about it that shapes the world in a particular way, but which can shape different aspects of the world. You can own stocks or flows of information, but far better to own the vector, the legal and technical protocols for making otherwise abundant information scarce.

If one takes a look at the top *Fortune 500* companies, it is surprising how many of them are really in the information business. I don't just mean the technology and telecommunication companies like Apple or Google or Verizon or Cisco or the drug companies like Pfizer. One could also think of the big banks as a subset of the vectoralist class rather than as "finance capital." They too are in the information asymmetry business. And as we learned in the 2008 crash, even the car companies are in the information business—they made more money from car loans than cars. The military–industrial sector is also in the information business. The companies that appear to sell actual things, like Nike, are really in the brand business. Walmart and Amazon compete with different models of the information logistics business.[21] Even the oil companies are in part at least in the information-about-the-geology-of-*possible*-oil-deposits business. Perhaps the vectoralist class is no longer emerging. Maybe it is the new dominant class.

One could make the case here that information was always central to capitalism and that this is just capitalism. To some extent, that may be the case. However, to even think that capitalism is about information is a fairly recent perspective. It ends up being a way of retrospectively seeing the whole course of capitalism in terms of something that only emerged as a concept and an instrumental reality as one of its late products.

The other point to clarify here is that there's a difference between information as a force of production and information as a *dominant* force of production. The vectoralist class doesn't need to own the other forces of production any more. Apple and Google don't actually make their own products. A sizable chunk of those they directly employ are not workers but hackers, people who come up with new information, whether of a technical or cultural kind, to be incorporated into products whose manufacture can be tendered out to a subordinate class of capitalists.

That might only be the case in the overdeveloped world where I happen to live.[22] Many of the world's peoples are not even workers but still peasants who are being turned into tenant farmers by the theft of their common land by a landlord class. Much of the world is also a giant sweatshop. The resistance of labor to capital is alive and well in China, India, Indonesia, and Vietnam. The older class antagonisms have not gone away. It's just that there's a new layer on top, trying to control them. Just as the capitalist class sought to dominate the landlord class as a subordinate ruling class, so too the vectoralist class tries to subordinate both landlords and capitalists by controlling the patents, the brands, the trademarks, the copyrights, but more importantly the logistics of the information vector.

The vector has also worked its way throughout the production process. This was already beginning in the so-called Fordist era. Some proposed naming it instead after the great Japanese companies that boomed in the mid to late twentieth century, such as Toyota and Sony. They were the ones who figured out how to extract not just labor but also information from the labor force. It turns out that to extract not only efficiency but also quality from industrial labor, it is best to incorporate the information held by those who know the labor process best—its workers.[23] That there is a hacker class at all is in part because workers have been stripped of the information they possess about the labor process itself.

In *Capital*, Marx mostly deals with an ideal-type political economy with two classes. But in his political writings it is clear that he understands social formations as hybrids of combined and overlapping modes of production.[24] His writing on France isn't just a grand confrontation between proletariat and bourgeoisie; the scene looms large with farmers, landlords, and peasants. So here I'm simply taking my cue from the political writings and thinking a matrix of six classes, three ruling and three subordinate. The dominant classes are landlords, capitalists, vectoralists. The subordinate classes are farmers, workers, hackers.

Now imagine all the possibilities of class alliance and conflict that this generates. It turns out that politics is much less about the relation between the friend and the enemy, and much more crucially about relations among *nonfriends* and *nonenemies*.[25] It's about shifting alliances of convenience between heterogeneous class interests. It's about conflicts that can take many forms, only some of them open, many of them discreet.

So how is this worse than capitalism? The vectoral infrastructure throws all of the world into the engine of commodification, meanwhile modifying the commodity form itself. There is nothing that can't be tagged and captured through information about it and considered a variable in the simulations that drive resource extraction and processing.[26] Quite simply, we have run out of world to commodify. And now commodification can only cannibalize its own means of existence, both natural and social. It's like that Marx Brothers film where the train runs out of firewood, so the carriages themselves have to be hacked to pieces and fed to the fire to keep it moving, until nothing but the bare bogies are left.[27]

It is worse also in that rather than some acephalous *multitude*, they are complex class alliances and conflicts at play.[28] The trickiest part of it is the politics of the hacker class, which after all is the class most of us here reading and writing this stuff belong to. Yes, it appears as a "privileged" class, among those whom Bruce Robbins calls the *beneficiaries* of global relations of exploitation.[29] And it is a class that has a very hard time thinking its common interests, because the kinds of new information its various subfractions produce are all so different. We have a hard time thinking what the writer and the scientist and artist and the engineer have in common. Well, the vectoral class does not have that problem. What all of us make is intellectual property, which from its point of view is as equivalent and as tradable as pink goo.

The hacker class experiences extremes of a winner-take-all outcome of its efforts. On the one hand, fantastic careers and the spoils of some simulation of the old bourgeois lifestyle; on the other hand, precarious and part-time work, start-ups that go bust, and the making routine of our jobs by new algorithms—designed by others of our very own class. The hacker class was supposed to be a privileged one, shielded from proletarianization by its creativity and technical skill. But it too can be made casual and precarious.

A controversial ad campaign for the website Fiverr embodied all these contradictions. It played on the desire to quit one's lousy job and become a boss, by offering the pleasure of subjecting others to the tyranny one feels as a precarious creative or technical employee these days. The ads promise a way to hire versions of your old self who are "doers." The most notorious ad showed a black and white picture of a hollow-cheeked, sad-eyed young woman staring directly at the viewer: "You eat a coffee for lunch. You follow through on your follow through. Sleep deprivation is your drug of choice," it reads, concluding: "You might be a doer." Another slogan was "Nothing like a safe, reliable paycheck to crush your soul." And "How much did you make for your boss today?" The one I most often saw defaced read "White Collars Can Come With Leashes." The slogans appear under pictures of a "diverse" workforce, of course: the algorithm is in theory very tolerant about who it exploits.

The old dream of labor, that it could organize itself, is supposed to be dead. There can be no dream of the hacker class to self-organize in any way, whether like labor or in some other form. Such desires are unspeakable, even if they keep erupting in all sorts of interesting ways. Sanctioned desire is neatly summed up in the image and slogan of a cellphone company: "Boss Revolution." The image is of a raised fist, with a cellphone in it, in red. The only desire permissible is to become a boss, like Don Draper.

This has not stopped some interesting and promising signs of hacker self-organization in technical and creative industries, from the unionization of creatives at Vice Media to the Google walkout to refusal to work on border control or military projects across the tech industry.[30] Baby steps, to be sure; it is always a tough argument to propose common interests among subordinate classes. Counter-hegemony is hard. Hackers, like workers or farmers, are distracted by particular and local interests. As with other subordinate classes, class consciousness is rare among hackers. Most of us are rather reactionary, even in the nontechnical trades. But then class consciousness is always a rare and difficult thing. Unlike other identities, it has to be argued *contrary* to appearances.

The feeling of belonging to a class rarely extends beyond appearances. It appears that one is a "creative" or working in "tech," for example. There could be a myriad of such classes. As we shall see in Chapter 4, this self-understanding of class restricts itself to appearances and masks not an essence but a structural question as to how one's efforts end up being commodified and who reaps most of the benefit of that. The received ideas within which one is asked to think about one's identity don't help when it comes to thinking how one is located within an information political economy, one where the hidden side of appearances is not eternal essence, just things one usually doesn't see—the forces of production.

To come into an awareness of class is to speak another language. It is to refuse the terms that are given and seek other terms, other concepts. This can be difficult. I can tell you from experience: the American college students that I meet cannot even pronounce *bourgeoisie*, let alone conceptualize it. Everything it once meant culturally has evaporated. The outward signs and styles of the ruling class don't look bourgeois. Our new-style overlords only wear suits when called before Congress; otherwise they wear discreetly expensive t-shirts. You don't see them cutting ribbons at factory openings. They don't preach hard work and thrift; they preach creativity, mindfulness, and ethical consumption. The bourgeois culture with which generations of Marxist aesthetics had a love–hate relationship is effectively extinct. The ruling class is not what it used to be. Maybe it needs another name.

What is even harder is to name those whose location in the political economy of information is the making of new information. It isn't exactly labor, as it's not the same thing every day; it's a different thing every day. Output is not quantifiable in increments, although that won't stop the vectoralist class from trying. One popular attempt to describe them (us) was as the *creative class*.[31] More radical approaches have called what we do *immaterial labor* or *postfordist labor*, and us the *cognitariat*.[32] But there's something a bit mystifying about the language of creativity, something a bit idealist about the immaterial, something backward looking about just adding a modifier, and something of a rationalist bias in the category of cognition, given that the management of feelings can be part of our job description, too.[33]

I opted to call us the *hacker class*. Twenty years ago, that was perhaps too romantic a term, on the border of legality, outside the logic of commodification.[34] Now it has more exclusively criminal associations. If anything, it's an index of how much the vectoralist class has succeeded. It is all but inconceivable now that there could be an open-ended, playful, experimental approach to making the new appear out of the old in techniques of information that would not be entirely contained with the commodification and control of the information vector.

But just as the industrial working class retained a utopian feeling about what labor should be like from craft labor, so too it is possible to hold onto a feeling about what it's like to make elegance appear that wasn't there before with a technique for transforming information, and to do it on one's own time, with one's own goals and objectives.[35] That is what it might mean to *hack*. Some of the more compelling scenes in both *Mad Men* and *Halt and Catch Fire* try to find a televisual language for these joyful moments, caught though they are, as the narrative arc reminds us, within the commodification of information.

To think that one's class is the hacker class might now be not unlike repurposing the word *queer*, or any of the other negatively charged terms that those so designated reclaim with pride—just as Marx and Engels reclaimed the word *communist* from its denouncers in the opening poetic gambit of the *Manifesto*. That was an artful bit of *détournement*. They refunctioned found language from the common store, deleted false meaning, pasted in fresh ones. To clear a space for thought is to work in and against language, to put some pressure on it.

What if we took a more daring, modernist, defamiliarizing approach to writing theory? What if we asked of theory as a genre that it be as interesting, as strange, as poetically or narratively rich as we ask our other kinds of literature to be? What if we treated it not as *high theory*, with pretentions to legislate or interpret other genres, but as *low theory*, as something vulgar, common, even a bit rude —having no greater or lesser claim to speak of the world than any other?[36] It might be more fun to read. It might tell us something strange about the world. It might, just might, enable us to act in the world otherwise. A world in which the old faith in History is no more, but where there are histories that still might be made—in a pinch.

The end of the dominance of capitalism as a mode of production is not a subject that has received much useful attention. For its devotees, it has no end, as it is itself the end of History.[37] For its enemies, it can end only in Communism. If Communism—a state that exists mostly in the imaginal realm, always deferred into the future—has not prevailed, then this by definition must still be the reign of Capital. Let's pause for a moment over the ideological freight attached to this poetic conceit and its consequences: the present is defined mostly in terms of a hoped-for negation of it. Some theology!

If capitalism is to be of any use as a *historical* concept, then the question of its end has to remain an open one. The thought experiment as to whether it may already have been surpassed by another dominant mode ought at least to be one that can be posed. The concept of Capital is theological precisely to the extent that questions of its possible surpassing by other exploitative modes of production remain off limits. How then can a concept of capitalism be returned to its histories? By abandoning the duality of its essence and appearance.

Theories of the eternal quality of Capital's essence, its unity and identity through time, tend to focus on the analysis of the *relations* of production. One can extract from Marx's *Capital* a quite remarkable theoretical armature that appears in the negative through the critique of the theological concepts of bourgeois political economy. This conceptual armature is so robust that there are few phenomena that resist interpretation as surface appearances of these concepts when posited as a hidden essence. Two things slip from view in this procedure. First, that the bourgeois political economy that Marx took as the object of critique is now itself a museum piece.[38] Second, that in this focus on the relations of production, the forces of production receive very little attention. We don't spend enough time on how the brain-fryer is a different machine from the meat grinder.

This is something of a problem, as surely the dynamism of those forces of production under capitalism was one of the salient points of the theory in the first place. But where the relations of production can be understood theoretically, the forces of production cannot. They don't lend themselves to an abstract, conceptual overview by a master thinker within a genteel high theory. They can really only be known through the collaborative production of a critical theory sharing the experiences of many fields. That would include those with a knowledge of information technology, artificial intelligence, supply chain management, material science, computational biology, and much else besides. We're way past the steam engines that Marx was sketching in his notebooks.[39]

Is it not possible, then, that there have been sufficient transformations in the forces of production to break out of the fetters of a strictly capitalist mode of production? There are two versions of this question. One is looking for a theological justification for this appearance of something new as finally putting an end to the more troubling aspects of capitalism for vectoralist class apologetics. But the more salient version of the question might be to ask whether what has emerged, in addition to and laminated on top of a capitalist mode of production, is something qualitatively different, but which generates new forms of class domination, new forms of the extraction of surplus, even new kinds of class formation.

The emergence of information as a material force of production looked for a while like it might escape the confines of existing relations of production and that it could negate existing property forms. (I return to this topic in Chapter 4). It looked for a while as though the one thing that really could form the basis of the commons was information. It blew apart the old culture industry. Producers of information started to think not just about their craft or trade interests but about a class interest.

Or so it looked early in the twenty-first century when I wrote *A Hacker Manifesto*. What I did not anticipate was the emergence of a whole other technique for the capture of creation. While there are still elements among the ruling class that want to confine creation within ever stricter forms of private property, some took the opposite tack. Rather than police or restrict free creation, this other strategy was to move its capture to a more abstract level. The production of information can be outsourced to *free labor*, to people who work but need not even be paid, and the aggregate value of their production of information can then be captured and treated as a resource that can be monetized.[40]

This new kind of ruling class does not appropriate a quantity of surplus value so much as exploit an asymmetry of information. It gives, sometimes even as a gift, access to the location of a piece of information for which you are searching.[41] Or it lets you assemble your own social network. Or it lets you perform a particular financial transaction. Or it gives you coordinates on the planet and what can be found at that location. Or it will even tell you some things about your own DNA. Or it will provide a logistical infrastructure for your small business. But while you get that little piece of information, this ruling class gets all of that information in the aggregate. It exploits the asymmetry between the little you know and the aggregate it knows—an aggregate it collects based on information you were obliged to "volunteer."

In practice, this emergent ruling class of our time insists on the confinement of particular acts of creation within the property form and access to collective creative activity, from which to harvest information in the aggregate. This is the vectoralist class. If the capitalist class owns the means of production, the vectoralist class owns the vectors of information. They own the *extensive* vectors of communication, which traverse space. They own the *intensive* vectors of computation, which accelerate time. They own the copyrights, the patents, and the trademarks that capture attention or assign ownership to novel techniques. They own the logistic systems that manage and monitor the disposition and movement of any resource. They own the financial instruments that stand in for the value of every resource and that can be put out on markets to crowdsource the possible value of every possible future combination of those resources. They own the algorithms that rank and sort and assign particular information in particular circumstances.

This vectoralist class comes to dominate not just subordinate classes, but other ruling classes as well. Just as capital came to dominate landed property, subsuming its control over land in a more abstract and fungible property form, so too the vectoralist class has subsumed and outflanked capital in a more abstract form. The capitalist class finds itself at a disadvantage. Owning the means of production, labor materialized into capital in the sense of plant and equipment, is a rigid and long-term investment. Owning and controlling the vector, the hack of new information materialized into patents, copyrights, brands, proprietary logistics. It is more abstract, flexible, adaptive. It is not more rational, but it is more abstract. The vectoralist class monopolizes the crossroads where information traffics, feeding like Michel Serres's parasite on the buzz of information and noise at crucial junctures.[42]

The most obvious aspect of vectoral rule in everyday life is its monopoly of attention, although it is not reducible to this. As Yves Citton notes, in a world awash in digital data, what is rare is the attention paid to it.[43] Commanding attention through the ownership and control of brands, celebrities and media "properties" is the public face, the disintegrating spectacle, of vectoral economy.[44] In part, this descends from what was formerly the culture industry. But it is no longer an industry apart, commodified leisure. It's now integrated into the whole of production and consumption.

This brief sketch of the supersession of capitalism as a dominant mode has the advantage of enabling many of the features of contemporary life that are often treated as separate to appear as aspects of the same historical development. The rise of technology, financialization, neoliberalism, and biopolitics appear as effects of the same transformation of the forces of production, putting pressure on the relations of production, to the point where what bursts forth is a new ruling class formation.

In the usual historical narrative, by the end of the seventies, the forces of labor had fought capital to a standstill in the overdeveloped world.[45] In this story, financialization and neoliberalism come to the rescue. But how? What material means made financialization even possible? What underlying social forces enabled neoliberal ideas to even appear plausible as policy instruments? Why does this coincide with the apparent birth of "tech" as an industry sector?

In the thought experiment I am sketching, all of these developments fit together in a novel way. The capitalist class was searching for a way out of the impasse of confronting the demands of labor at a time when improvements of the old means of production no longer yielded much by way of a productivity increase. The capitalist class thought it found a way out by replacing labor with the vector and escaping along it. Globalization, deindustrialization, and outsourcing would enable it to be free from the power of labor to block the flows of production. The same information vector would enable not just a more abstract and flexible kind of production, but also of consumption, through the financialization of everyday life.[46] Workers as producers found their jobs had moved elsewhere; workers as consumers found their purchasing power restored—at least temporarily.

Here's the twist: what at first appeared to assist capital to defeat labor in the overdeveloped world was also a *defeat for capital*. The novel forces of production that enabled this outflanking of labor became themselves the new dominant forces of production. Power over the value chain moves from the ownership and control of the means of production to ownership and control of the vectors of information. Whole new industries arose, as did whole new corporations—the so-called tech sector. But actually all corporations become increasingly organized around the ownership and control of information.

Control over the value chain through ownership of the information vector extends even into life itself. This is not the least reason, incidentally, that it is no longer helpful to posit the vitalism of living labor against capital as dead labor.[47] Not capital but the vector enters the flesh and commands it, and not just as meat, but also as information, through monitoring its states, through modifying its functions with drugs that alter chemical signals, through patenting aspects of life as design.[48] What is at stake is neither a *bios* nor a *polis* but a regime of property in information extending into the organism. The novel forces of production as they have emerged in our time are also forces of reproduction and forces of circulation.

The power of the vectoralist class is not cognitive; nor is it a power over the general intellect.[49] It thrives just as well on noise, on volatility, on bad information as it does on any kind of intelligence or reason.[50] It reaches just as far into the corporeality and even sexuality of the human as it does into the intellect.[51] The forms of artificial computational order it is creating are not extensions or imitations of human cognition but something else entirely.[52]

One cannot interpret the strangeness of this mode of production using the received hermeneutic conceptual categories, derived as they are from a critique of the relations of production of nineteenth-century steam-powered capitalism. Indeed, one sees now how incomplete Marx's critique was and remains. Even his critical understanding of capitalism is still thinking capitalism metaphorically as like a giant, dysfunctional steam engine, set to blow at any moment from unregulated internal pressures.[53] Marx is not able to think critically about information in the contemporary sense of the concept because it is not one that the forces of production of his time have yet produced.

Marx found what was absent in the theories of Capital in his time. He lifted the veil between exchange and production and found the exploited labor that makes it. He wrote the heresy that Capital is dead labor—congealed pink goo—and he went on to write from the point of view of the labor that capital exploits. So: let's go looking for what is absent in theories of both Capital and information in our time. Let's find that peculiar class who own and control information. Let's find the exploited class or classes that make it and are subjected to it. In vulgar terms: the capitalist class eats our bodies, the vectoralist class eats our brains.

Returning this thought experiment to the present, one might then be able to think the historical specificity of the contemporary moment. This, after all, was Marx's great achievement. He thought *his* moment. His present did not look to him like his past. It had novel features that called into being concepts adequate to the situation. Which leaves us with the paradoxical and provocative thought that any theory in which the present appears as in essence the same as the past of Marx's time, only different in a few matters of appearance, can't really be a "Marxist" one, as such fidelity is necessarily a betrayal of his achievement. Debord: "And theories are made to die in the war of time."[54]

Perhaps we can leave such theological questions to the faithful, who are in any case an embattled and diminished band. Instead, here is a research agenda: what are the current forces of production, and how can they be understood (in a preliminary way) under a modest set of concepts? How do those forces of production give rise to contemporary forms of class power, and how has that power in turn shaped the particular form those forces of production have taken? At what points might the subordinate classes, obliged to live within the world those forces of production make in the interests of those ruling class, be able to assert agency and autonomy? What other world is still possible, given the damage this general economy has done to the world, with the means that it has hitherto developed?[55]

3

The Forces of Production

We work to communicate to commune
but must do so in a circuit
of graduated expropriation.

—Jonathan Beller

The first and last question that usually comes up about technology is whether it is a good or a bad thing. This can apply both to particular technologies and to technology in general. Marx can readily be recruited to either side of this argument, either through quoting selectively, picking the Marx of a particular period, or extracting a particular perspective out of his work at the expense of the dialectical and poetical play at work in his corpus. Marx has a lot of uses on the technology question. He is an all-purpose tool.

Marx might also offer "tools" for thinking a bit more critically about technology. Do we have to subject technology to a moral decision only, as good or bad? How does this technology appear as a thing apart that one could contemplate and judge? From what kind of genteel point of view does it seem something separate? What range of things are we thinking of as *technical*, anyway?

Starting from the last of those questions, it is important to situate

Marx in his own times. What we now think of as technology was for Marx more a question of the machine. His was an era of steam, which powered factories, railways, shipping, and the printing presses of the newspapers for which he wrote.[1] It was an era of telegraphy, but before the wide distribution of electric power, or the rise of modern chemistry, particle physics, genetics, climate science, or information science. Marx did his best to keep up with the scientific and technical developments of his time, but that was more Engels's job. Marx's knowledge of how the physical world works, and hence his materialism, stops short at a certain historical threshold.[2]

Nevertheless, Marx makes important steps toward thinking technology as a set of things that can be grasped with a concept. Particularly in the *Grundrisse*, he starts to write about technology beyond the moral decision of whether it is good or bad.[3] He starts to write of it as having a range of possibilities, as something that has, as one might say in a more modern idiom, "affordances." Consistent with the rest of his thinking, Marx comes to understand technology not as having an essence, but as something emerging out of particular historical circumstances.

This gave him a way to think beyond the curious way that technology appears as something separate. Technology is intimately connected on the one hand to the human and on the other to the nonhuman. Indeed, technology may be the inhuman zone where distinctions between the human and the nonhuman, not to mention anxieties about their permeability, originate. Among other things, technology mediates senses of the human to the human.

To take up just the first of these connections for now: Marx could see technology as connected to the human in a double way. To put it simply: the *content* of technology is labor; the *form* of technology is capital. It is living labor that makes technology; technology is congealed dead labor—pink goo—that then returns to confront the worker in the form of capital. The form of technology is capital, in that it is shaped by the objective of extracting value from labor (and from nature) as efficiently as possible.

As particular capitalist firms compete with each other, they reach for labor-saving devices to increase output and drive down costs, replacing living labor with dead labor, but in the long run putting a squeeze on profits, as surplus value is extracted from exploiting human labor alone. The form of technology is capital in a second sense, too. Not all decisions that capital makes about technical change in the workplace are, strictly speaking, economic. Capital may also implement technical change that takes power away from the worker at the point of production.[4]

Technology is not a separate thing, then. It is intimate to the human, in a bifurcated way: capital in form is capital; in content, it is labor. Labor makes the machine, but not in the design of its own choosing. There is a parallel connection, on the other side, to the nonhuman, to nature. Technology is made of, and remakes, nature itself. Technology's content is sensuous materiality, iron and coal and so forth, mixed with labor; its form is once again the form of capital. Rimbaud: "If the brass awakens as a horn, it's not to blame."[5]

One can thus connect Marx's writing on technology to his writing on nature. Besides the tension between the points of view of technology as labor in content but capital in form, there is a second distinction running through Marx's work, connected with his practice of forming concepts negatively, through the *détournement* of bourgeois language. At different times, Marx worked on the critique of different kinds of bourgeois thinkers.[6] The various ideas he worked to negate leave an imprint on the concepts that result.

In the *Grundrisse*, Marx is working on a critique of a Hegelian conception of labor as spirit, as that which engages and shapes the world, humanizing the world, while making the human more "worldly." In

Capital, Marx was also working in and against the less well-known scientific materialism in vogue in Germany after the failure of the 1848 revolutions.[7] From this, Marx took a thermodynamic concept of labor as an expenditure of energy and an image of capitalism as a gigantic steam engine that would either break down or run down.[8]

Even before the *Grundrisse* notebooks were widely known, this tension in Marx produced two distinct approaches to thinking about technology. The more genteel approach thought it possible to produce an adequate concept of technology with the critical tools of philosophy alone. Meanwhile, vulgar approaches emerged that were more involved in practices connected to scientific and technical knowledge upon which technology actually works. The rapid development of the forces of production generated a combinatory of approaches to both the question of what technology is, but also to what Marxism itself could be or become. Here I'll briefly map both of these fields.

First, let's make a grid with two axes to map four kinds of Marxist theorists of technology: those who view it negatively, as capitalist in form; those who view it positively, as labor in content. Then there are those who view it philosophically, whether for or against it; those who view it more scientifically, whether for or against it. While this does not account for all of the vast literature on technology after Marx, it does provide a basic orientation within this combinatory of possibilities.

Those with a more affirmative and vulgarly scientific view of technology often take Engels as their point of departure. In the intellectual division of labor between them, Engels more than Marx took on research into scientific topics, polemics with the scientific ideologies of his time, and the question of whether there could even be a dialectics of nature.[9] Engels lived long enough to see the sciences becoming systematically organized as a source of competitive advantage in fields such as the chemical industry, so the question of science and its impact on the development of the forces of production was no mere intellectual question.[10]

The rise of modern physics provoked a profound crisis among Marxists.[11] If *materialism* is at base a doctrine of the sole reality of the material world, then it matters what matter is actually made of, and it matters how this is known. Do quantum mechanics and general relativity confirm or refute the Marxist philosophy of dialectical materialism? Or does dialectical materialism refute modern science? While the latter position had its proponents among the philosophers, the development of Marxism turned more on how Marxism could be interpreted as having been compatible with modern physics even before it existed.[12]

This brings me to the second grid, which maps some responses to changing technology as to what Marxism itself might be or become in such a situation. To simplify things, they can be mapped onto a grid with four quadrants, one axis of which is whether Marxism is treated as a first philosophy that describes the world, or has a more limited role as something like a method for organizing practices of knowledge. The other axis is once again as to whether this is to be approached in a vulgar or a genteel manner.

The genteel half of the map would include those who (like the later Lukács) make ontological claims within Marxism, and those who (like the young Althusser) treat it more as a method for organizing practices, but still a philosophical method.[13] Among the vulgarians would be the keepers of orthodox, Soviet-approved dialectical materialist theory, who accept that it makes claims about the world but of a more "scientific" than philosophical kind. It would also include those like J. B. S. Haldane who restrict Marxism to being a method for organizing research, but of a more empiricist stripe than it would later appear in Althusser. And it would also include Alexander Bogdanov, who dispenses with the whole notion of a dialectical materialist philosophy.[14]

Reformulated as a method for organizing knowledge practices, Marxism could be quite compatible with scientific work and could provide procedures for thinking about the place of science within capitalism. This was the basic orientation of the left wing of the Social Relations of Science movement, which was strongest in Britain between the thirties and the fifties.[15] This orientation maintained a positive outlook on the potentials of technology, as science applied to the rationalization of social production. Yet it was at the same time highly critical of the subordination of science and technology to the capitalist monopoly firm and the imperialist and militarist state.[16]

In terms of their class origins, many of the leading lights of the Social Relations of Science movement were quite genteel. (J. D. Bernal was the son of an Irish landowner; Haldane was from the titled gentry.) Their Marxism was vulgar in other ways. They were inclined to think that the development of the forces of production was a driving force in history. This was not unconnected to their work in the sciences, where they witnessed first-hand the dynamic creativity of applied science and the limited way this was absorbed by capital.

Their work has rather fallen out of the canon in favor of more genteel Marxist approaches, which is a shame, as it was particularly strong on the study of changes in the forces of production. In *Science in History*, Bernal showed how science (broadly conceived) played a critical role in the economic and social organization of all societies. V. Gordon Childe showed how the mode of production of even ancient societies sets limits to how knowledge and technology developed. Joseph Needham systematically refuted the assumption that science was somehow part of some western rational essence. Until modern times science and technology developed more fully in China than in the West.[17]

In their analysis of the capitalism of their time, they slip between the agency of labor and the agency of science, held together by one of their preferred terms for their own class location, that of the *scientific worker*. What this left unclear is whether the scientist is part of the working class or is external but potentially allied to organized labor. Latent in the formulation is the possibility to conceive of a new kind of class agent, who is neither labor nor capital. What I find here is an early intimation of one aspect of an emerging hacker class.

One of the sources of the radicalism of this group was the experience of laboratory life itself. The sciences in which they had this experience were rising fields in the early twentieth century such as x-ray crystallography, biochemistry, and genetics. They practiced science at a transitional moment, after the era in which science was the pastime of gentlemen and before the rise of big science.[18] The element of free, self-directed discovery in their practice was qualified and hemmed in on all sides, but it was palpable nonetheless. This hint of a life without alienation provided part of the leverage against what science was becoming as its value for corporate and military power was increasingly appreciated.

Red science did not survive the Cold War, however. Influential figures such as Bernal and Needham found themselves sidelined, and younger researchers kept their heads down. It is ironic that Foucault favorably contrasts J. Robert Oppenheimer (the *specific intellectual*) to Jean-Paul Sartre (the *general intellectual*). The former is supposedly a better practice because his public statements draw directly and narrowly on his expertise in nuclear physics. What Foucault downplays is how the Cold War left progressive scientists with no choice other than to present themselves as apolitical servants of ethical causes, arguing about good and bad technology rather than forwarding the analysis of the forces of production as a historical agent.[19]

Of course there have been Marxist scientists, even significant ones, despite the Cold War.[20] But there has been little since the fifties to match the influence of the Social Relations of Science movement.

However, something like it happened later in information science. Richard Stallman, a "red diaper baby" and founder of the free software movement, brought some of his mother's stubborn militancy to the possibilities and limits of computer science. It was Stallman who made the strongest connection between the everyday life of the hacker and the struggle in and against the commodification of information science.[21]

Here theorists and activists from the sciences connect to those from the arts who, like Asger Jorn, tried to think the agency of form-making as distinct from capital, but also from labor, which works to fill pregiven forms with content. The producers of both form and content might both then be allied in their struggle against subordination to the regime of the commodity.[22] It is an alliance that, while rare, has in certain situations been realized.[23]

What Jorn ironically called the *creative elite* and what Bernal and others call the *scientific worker* seem to me to be two aspects of what will become the hacker class. This class appears when both scientific form-discovering and aesthetic form-making can be extracted and valued as instances of the same thing, as intellectual property, by a new kind of ruling class. The new ruling class understands this not as a way to maintain the competitive advantage of an existing manufacturing industry, but as a whole other kind of industry in its own right, one that can dominate manufacturing through the control of information. (I will return to questions of class in Chapter 4.)

So far I've looked at an affirmative and scientific approach to technology. This has a parallel in a more philosophical but also affirmative school of thought. An influential version of this arises out of the autonomist Marxism of postwar Italy.[24] Its starting point is a reading of Marx's *Grundrisse* rather than *Capital*. The key concept extracted from *Grundrisse* is based on something Marx says, almost in passing, about the *general intellect*.[25] The rising complexity of capitalist organization comes increasingly to depend not just on the exploitation of particular labors, but on the socialization of knowledge, embedded into the form of technology as general intellect. Thus, the socialization of labor is already partly achieved, and it remains only to throw off the last vestiges of an obsolete private property form.

It is more common for philosophically based Marxist theories of technology to be critical of it. Lukács extended the Marxist theory of alienation into the technical form itself. Costas Axelos combined Marx with Heidegger, resulting in a critique not of the form of technology under capitalism, but the form of technology itself.[26] Guy Debord extended Lukács's critique of the alienating form of technology in the sphere of production to the sphere of consumption and its reigning images, which he called the *spectacle*.[27] Both Lukács and Debord saw Marxist philosophy as a theory of the totality. In Lukács, reified labor, of which bourgeois science is an aspect, falls short of the totality, while in Debord the spectacle falsifies the totality itself.

A rather more interesting case of genteel Marxism is Herbert Marcuse, who extended Lukács's theory of reification to a nightmare view of technocratic enclosure. But there was always the possibility of a utopian dimension to technology in Marcuse, if it could be freed from the limited rationality of means and ends. As his contemporary interpreter Andrew Feenberg points out, he drew on an unlikely source for this: Gilbert Simondon. In Simondon, Marcuse found the possibility of another rationality, one perhaps even more technical, in which inhuman technical forms might co-evolve with the human.[28]

The more scientifically trained have often been connected to the more affirmative view of technology as product of labor and means of achieving the expansion of social production that might satisfy social needs without exploitation. But there have also been critical voices. Barry Commoner studied biology and took Bernal as his inspiration, but became a critic of technology and a proponent of a form of ecological socialism.[29] The more one knows about natural science, the more one can find the damage the commodity form does it.

Donna Haraway also trained as a biologist. Starting in part from Needham, she complicates the concept of technology as capital in form and labor in content. Her use of the figure of the *cyborg* as a "political myth" (or thought experiment) helps us think of hybrid, inhuman agencies, with no neat separation of human and nonhuman actors. She includes other species besides humans in the organization of production and control.[30]

While sometimes thought of within the genres of feminist or science studies or media studies, I want to stress the vulgar-Marxist aspect of Haraway.[31] She brings a critical approach to bear on a scientific literature surely as powerful in our time as political economy was in Marx's: the life sciences. Like Marx, she shows how these are at one and the same time actual sciences and yet ones limited by the basic metaphors emanating from the forms of production and reproduction of their times. She asks vulgar questions about how gender and sexuality are caught up in productive and reproductive labor—and even in relations that are not obviously either. Haraway's writing is also vulgar in another sense, in that the cyborg is among other things a kind of popular countermyth. Buried within the knotty writing and witty *détournement* of that text is a nugget of Marxist-feminist utopian writing.

In related work, the physicist Karen Barad has revived an approach to science studies that could justifiably be considered Marxist. Based on a reading of Neils Bohr, she offers a theory of *agential realism*, which considers more things to be actors in the production of knowledge besides labor, scientific labor, and what Haraway called the *multi-species muddle*. Here even subatomic phenomena can be understood as agents. Barad pays close attention to the role of the *apparatus* in science.[32] The apparatus can be thought of as discrete parts of the forces of production. It is also what I call the *inhuman*, the indeterminate zone where what Barad calls the *cut* is made that distinguishes the human from the nonhuman.

Also partly under the influence of Haraway, Paul B. Préciado questions the emphasis on the *general intellect* in autonomist Marxism and its descendants, from the point of view of the kinds of technologized bodies produced by contemporary pharmaceuticals.[33] The gendered human body itself is partly inhuman, a technically augmented and chemically sustained artifact. The critical agent in this scenario is less the scientific worker and more a loose alliance do-it-yourself, self-organized, gender hacking punks and various kinds of body-workers, including sex workers, transgender artists and activists.[34]

My own connection to these questions comes from spending much of the nineties immersed in media avant-gardes that tried to build critical practices out of a low-tech, punk approach to digital technologies.[35] Where Adorno or Pasolini occupied residual cultural spaces that predated commodification, here was an instance of an emerging one that nobody had quite figured out how to subsume into a "business model." This gave rise organically to a kind of low theory that tried to produce concepts that could keep up with the mutations in information technology wending their way throughout the whole consumption, circulation, and production cycle.

The Internet came out of the university and took capital by surprise. While many a scholar was writing genteel Marxist theory in the humanities, in information science a whole new mode of production was germinating. It had already transformed much of the sciences. By the nineties there was enough cheap technology around to take a punk approach and develop new theories and practices with and about it. I'll mention just two examples, starting with Dmytri Kleiner's détourned text, the *Telekommunist Manifesto*.[36]

Kleiner's starting point is the transformation of the forces of production and the pressure this put on the relations of production. Cheap computation plus the Internet vector was supposed to make capitalism more efficient and enable capital to route around the power of workers at the point of production. It did all that, but it also opened the prospect of self-organized peer-to-peer production.[37] There really could have been a *telecommunism* ("tele" = "at a distance"). Autonomous producers could cheaply and easily communicate and coordinate. This was a possibility that had to be foreclosed to enable a new kind of capture of the surplus by the rising ruling class that I call the *vectoralist class*.

On the technical level, what developed in place of a peer-to-peer network was a client–server network, built around privately owned hubs—what Benjamin Bratton calls *stacks*.[38] Meanwhile, states engaged each other in trade agreements, which produced transnational regimes of intellectual property designed to secure surplus information within novel forms of private property. The free creation of information would be alternately policed and encouraged: policed where it infringed on corporate monopolies; encouraged where free labor or nonlabor could be captured as information that had value. We now have the information commons as a form of disintegrated spectacle, owned by the vectoralist class. What Kleiner advocates as a counterstrategy is what he calls *venture communism*: "Politics is not a battle of ideas it is a battle of capacities."[39] The hacker class has to create its own autonomous forms.

"A specter is haunting the net, the specter of communism."[40] Like Kleiner, Richard Barbrook (and his collaborator, the late Andy Cameron) emerged out of the intersection of media activism and practice and produced illuminating *détournements* of Marxist texts as a way to grasp the nineties situation. Barbrook took the point of view of what he called *digital artisans* against the rise of the *virtual class*.[41]

72

What was particularly useful in these polemical texts was the identification of the *California Ideology* as the worldview of this emerging ruling class, one whose success is to be measured by the sad fact that even critics of "bad technology" take it for gospel.

The California Ideology emerged out of seemingly progressive movements of the counterculture in California in the mid to late twentieth century.[42] Once again, repression played a role. Black militants of this period were systematically murdered or imprisoned.[43] To give just one example, Angela Davis survived a criminal trial and was fired from her teaching job. Shorn of its more radical edge, the counterculture became merely cultural, and its anti-state posture made its peace with free market libertarian enthusiasms. Like the worldviews of capital under feudalism, the California Ideology promised a universal liberation, which turned out on its ascendency to be just that of a new ruling class.

Drawing on the historical vision of the lapsed socialist Alvin Toffler, the California Ideology proposed a world in which technology itself was the sole transformative force of history.[44] The hero of this epical-poetical myth was the entrepreneur, who single-handedly battles against labor, state, and culture to unleash the supposedly "natural" force of technology. Once unbound, technology will show itself to be inherently the vehicle of free markets and a return to Jeffersonian democracy.[45] Hence, technology is good in essence.

Barbrook follows Marx in seeking out the internal contradictions in this emerging ruling class ideology. He notes the irony of the retro-futurist celebration of Thomas Jefferson as the patron saint of yeoman democracy that fails to mention that he was a slaveholder.[46] Unfortunately, many of the tech-pundits of today lack Barbrook's wit and historical acumen, and they take much of the California Ideology for granted. The result is a sort of conspiracy theory, in which the public was allegedly duped by a cabal of "Silicon Valley" entrepreneurs. To mask their intention to unleash powerful tools of monopoly and political control, they lulled everyone into thinking technology was in essence good when it is in essence bad.

As Barbrook points out, the development of the forces of production is not magically called into being from the brains of business geniuses. In the case of Silicon Valley, it took a massive amount of state funding, passing through university research labs.[47] It may at one point have been quite possible that these developments could have led to a digital agora or commons as well as (or as an alternative to) new forms of class power based on information asymmetries and the surveillance state. What gets erased in both moral fables about technology, the one where its essence is good and the one where its essence is bad, is the struggle over the form the technologies of Internet would take.

Both Barbrook and Kleiner get critical purchase through a *détournement* of classic Marx texts, erasing terms that spoke to the past, replacing them with a language saturated in the emerging class struggles of the times. Interestingly, both deployed the modifier, but they added it not to Capital but to their concepts of what might come into being within and against it to negate it: Kleiner's *telekommunism* and Barbrook's *cybercommunism*. I read this now as a useful transitional tactic for working in and against the combinatory of terms inherited from former historical conflicts, on its way to a theory of the present situation, wherein the development of the forces of production might start to escape the porous bounds of the relations of production through unanticipated cracks.

In the nineties it still seemed possible to shape a different future for the Internet, and there were many struggles around its emerging form: technical, political, legal, and cultural. We won some battles; we lost the war. Like the progressive wing of the Social Relations of Science, this was in the end a defeated movement. But that is no reason to pretend it didn't exist. Rather, there's work to be done to narrate and analyze the struggles of that time and those that continue as relatively novel expressions of what kinds of worlds are possible in and against the forces of production of these times.[48]

Marx saw capitalism as evidence in the negative that the problem of material scarcity was potentially solvable. We now see that information scarcity is in principle solved already. In both cases, we get critical leverage, in the first case, on the persistence on exploitation; in the second, on the persistence of disinformation, noise, and information asymmetry. Once again, the means are at hand to solve these problems, but the class nature of the existing relations of production are a fetter on the forces of production. Only it is not just the capitalist class that is a fetter on development this time—it is the vectoralist class as well. But to think of that as a problem means not only to pay attention to the forces of production, it is to look again at the class relations they both generate and are structured within. What is good or bad about technology is the outcome of class conflict over its form and between more than two classes.

4

The Class Location Blues

> It is a universal law that before it disappears,
> every class must first disgrace itself completely.
>
> —Aimé Césaire

A reminder of the thought experiment that threads through these chapters: What if this was no longer capitalism, but something worse? Could we approach this now by describing relations of exploitation and domination in the present, starting with the emerging features, and work back and out and up from that? This chapter plays mostly with the *sociological imagination*.[1] This is the ability to conceptualize the problem *synchronically*, as if we could slice through the social formation of the present and look at its anatomy, rather than *diachronically*, in terms of patterns of development through time (a topic discussed in Chapter 5, a historical fantasia).

Since the sociology we are playing with is vulgar Marxist, our imagination might be drawn initially to some features of the *forces* of production. It is still the case that extracting useful organic and inorganic matter from the earth is the basis of social existence. And it is still the case that applying vast amounts of energy in the form of fossil fuels and labor to that base matter is still how the endless array of commodities around us come into existence. But both of those processes seem these days to be subordinated to a third form of relation. At the smallest and largest scales, so much of primary production and secondary manufacturing seems to be controlled by rapid flows, extensive archives and complex algorithms whose concrete existence is in a tertiary form—that of information.

The forces of production that instrumentalize information extend all the way into the production process, whether in the form of industrial robotics or the detailed and constant surveillance of living labor. They extend all the way out to global networks of measurement, command, and control that work in real time. These networks of information subsume not only inorganic and organic matter and energy in their web but also the human as "user," who becomes a producer of information even when not working. The value of information can be extracted even from free labor.

The relations of production seem to evolve to enclose these forces in rather novel extensions of the private property form. Wittgenstein's contribution to communism was his robust proof of the proposition that there is no private language, but in our time, privatized languages are everywhere.[2] And not just languages: Images, codes, algorithms, even genes can become private property, and in turn private property shapes what we imagine the limits and possibilities of this information to be.

Information is a relation between novelty and repetition, noise and order.[3] Novelty is extracted from a class whose efforts are hardly described by the category of labor, for the simple reason that while labor repeats an action whose form is given in advance, the whole point of these actions is to produce unique instances of such forms in the first place. Alongside the worker is the figure of the hacker, producer not of repeated content but of novel form, and form which more often than not ends up being someone else's property.

One has to ask whether the ruling class presiding over this mode of production is still adequately described as capitalist.[4] It seems no longer necessary to directly own the means of production. A remarkable amount of the valuation of the leading companies of our time consists not of tangible assets, but rather of information. A company is its brands, its patents, its trademarks, its reputation, its logistics, and perhaps above all its distinctive practices of evaluating information itself.

Some like to talk as if one could just add an adjective or two to capitalism and describe all this, but we have already rejected that option as uninteresting poetry. Maybe it's not the same old familiar endless essence of capitalism cloaked in new appearances. For instance, call it finance capitalism if you like, but perhaps the rise of finance is really just a symptom. Yann Moulier Boutang invites us to see finance as something other than speculative or fictive excess.[5] It has to do with the whole problem of exchange value in an age where the forces of production are extensively and intensively controlled by information: nobody knows what anything is worth. Financialization is a perverse socializing of the problem of the uncertainty of information about value.

So let's think of it as a postcapitalist mode of production, with a ruling class of a different kind, the vectoralist class. Their power does not lie in directly owning the means of production, as the capitalist class does. Nor does it lie in owning agricultural land, as the capitalists' old enemy, the landlord class, does. And just as there was conflict between capitalist and landlord, so now there is conflict between capitalist and vectoralist. Capital is dead; long live the vectoralist class.

It was with new forces of production that Capital defeated labor in the late twentieth century. Like the sorcerer's apprentice, Capital summoned up forces it could not restrain or control. Capital in turn finds itself struggling against a rising class that provided the very means of that victory. If one can use an information infrastructure to route around labor's power to block the production process, one can use the same means to make capitalist producers compete with each other on a global scale.[6]

This defamiliarized language for the information political economy has one small merit. It enables one to tell a fairly coherent story about what happened between the seventies and now. For comparison, let's look at some of the more characteristic language about that period. My example here is the work of the late Erik Olin Wright, collected in *Understanding Class*.[7] I want to pay close attention to Wright for two reasons. First, Wright upholds a Marxist approach to class, insisting on not only the salience of class as a key category of social thought, but of a specifically Marxist understanding of the concept. Second, while agreeing with Wright up to this point, I want to see if a *détournement* of his writing can be adapted to thinking the emergence of new classes.

But first, let's dip briefly into the *diachronic*, or historical, understanding of capitalism. I want to dissent from the "just-so" story Wright tells about how we got to the present moment. Wright: "The combination of globalization and financialization meant that from the early 1980s the interests of the wealthiest and most powerful segments of the capitalist class in many developed capitalist countries, perhaps especially in the United States, became increasingly anchored in global financial transactions and speculation and less connected to the economic conditions and rhythms of their national bases or any other specific geographical location."[8] This sentence, stripped of its decoration, basically says: the cause of financialization is financialization, and the cause of globalization is globalization.

Wright speaks of a period when "global competition intensified," where there was the "integration of commodity chains and production chains" and the "emergence of a global labor force" and even the "dramatic financialization of capitalist economies."[9] With what means? By whom? These are phrases from sentences that don't consistently link subjects to objects and which are fond of passive verbs. This theory of history can be summed up as: shit happens.

Of course, these are statements Wright adopts from a consensus language. We have all agreed to talk about financialization as if it just happened, without requiring actual material practices and techniques.[10] We have all agreed to talk about neoliberalism as if that described an actual agency at work that causes things to happen.[11] We have decided not to be Marxists, in other words. We have decided not to subject the language of the times to its own critical pressure. Marx certainly did not take the abstract nouns of the ruling ideology of his era as a given. Nor did he think that ideas were causative.

Let's look at Wright again, whose work is in many other respects a salutary example of how to bring analytic rigor to the Marxist tradition. He writes: "At the very heart of Marxism as a social theory is the idea of emancipatory alternatives to capitalism." And: "Unless one retains some coherent idea of there being an alternative to capitalism, a Marxist class analysis loses its central anchor."[12] Even in this social-scientific version of the Marxist tradition we're not far from the combinatory, in which History can only be understood through an ahistorical concept of Capital. Emancipation is thought negatively as emancipation from capitalism. Therefore, the negative *of* emancipation *must* be capitalism.

Of course, there's plenty of evidence for this still being capitalism or mostly capitalism. The question would be whether an additional mode of production is emerging and whether it is qualitatively different enough to call it something else. The problem with an inherited concept, like inherited money, is that we didn't make it ourselves and come to take it for granted. Maybe we need a bit of good old Brechtian alienation-effect even from heirloom concepts like "capitalism."[13]

What if we thought about a mode of production emerging after capitalism that is even worse? As an example of how one might conduct a thought experiment, I turn again to Erik Olin Wright. He asks: what can a Marxist concept of class bring to theoretical and empirical work that thinks class as stratification, or which uses class concepts drawn more from the work of Max Weber or Emile Durkheim? Wright deftly shows what a Marxist concept of class can do when endless capitalism is a given. The additional question I want to ask is this: What happens if we take away the assumption that this is still the same old capitalism?

Wright has mercifully given up genteel Marxism's "paradigm aspiration"[14] wherein Marxism is superior to all the social sciences because it has a superior problematic or method. Instead, Wright makes two sorts of claims, which rest somewhere on a continuum between sovereignty and collaboration. The modest claim is that one can connect Marxist work to other kinds of sociology. Each has its perspective and they illuminate each other. The stronger claim is that the Marxist perspective is a bigger picture, which shows something about the world and history that is beyond the reach of other approaches.

Here he does for social theory what Fredric Jameson does for literary theory or Perry Anderson for historical thought: make the claim that Marxism offers the point of view from which to interpret and synthesize other bodies of work. This then appears as the point of view not of the working class but of the totality itself. If Jameson's famous watchwords are "always historicize!" then Wright's might be "always socioligize!" where that means to adopt the point of view of a social formation riven by relations of class exploitation and domination as the outer limits of the macroscopic perspective.[15]

In one of his brilliant summaries, Wright argues that Durkheimian, Weberian, and Marxist approaches operate on different scales of what

I would call the *gamespace* of the contemporary social formation.[16] These are the *situational*, the *institutional*, and the *systemic* scales. The Durkheimian approach is situational and is about small-scale moves within the game. The Weberian approach is institutional and is about medium-scale rules of the game. The Marxist approach is systemic and is about a large-scale change of the game.

All of these approaches involve class relations that generate class actors who have at least partially conscious intentions, whether it is to make moves that advance them, or contest rules of the game that might advantage their class, or to change the whole game to another game. My question would be about the *class unconscious*. Perhaps a player other than the working class changed the game, as the forces of production push forward into new relations of production, with which our superstructural languages for describing class structure have yet to catch up.

Wright thinks that the opportunity for game-changing by the working class, for overthrowing capitalism, is not present. "One way of interpreting the history of the past half-century is that there has been a gradual shift in the levels of the game at which, for many analysts, class analysis seems most relevant."[17] Hence it makes sense to reach out to the Weberians (whose scholarly interests are at the level of contesting the rules of the game rather than changing it) and even to the Durkheimians (whose focus is on the moves actors get to make within given rules of the game). Wright's overall aim is to concatenate these three approaches as appropriate to different scales, with Marx speaking to the larger and more visionary scale.

This is a useful retort to the "death of class" counternarrative.[18] Wright offers a supple class analysis and backs it up with actual results —with the precision of a social science. His concept of class has three axes: property, authority, expertise. His view of class structure offers class locations at three levels, which do not always neatly overlap.

Relations of property generate the class locations of employers, petit-bourgeois, and employees. *Relations of authority* generate the locations of managers, supervisors, and the supervised and managed. *Relations of expertise* generate the locations of professionals, the skilled, and the nonskilled.

He is interested in the permeability of class boundaries, so he looks at three kinds of class connection: intergenerational mobility, cross-class friendship, and cross-class households. He finds the property boundary the least permeable (a result that won't surprise Marxists). Class connections between workers and employers are limited. The boundary between the employee and the petit bourgeois is more permeable. Wright frankly acknowledges that in the United States, racial boundaries may be even less permeable, but that does not negate the usefulness of the category of class. Class is only a modest predictor. And yet "class often performs as well or better than many other social structural variables in predicting a variety of aspects of attitudes."[19]

Let's compare this to perspectives rooted in Durkheim and Weber. In Durkheimian analyses of class, occupations are the unit of analysis.[20] They see class homogeneity only at the micro, occupational level, not in "big" concepts of class. It's more about actual labor markets and how they define occupations. Such occupations act on behalf of members, extract rents if they can, and shape life chances. For them, even academic sociologists and economists count as different "classes." Which might be the beginnings of an approach to how academics, at a time when their life chances are diminishing and their means of opportunity hoarding are failing, cannot quite come together and act on shared interests. Even Marxists in different fields become alienated from each other in this Durkheimian world of micro-classes.

The Durkheimian approach focuses on selection and self-selection into closed groups who interact more with each other than with other groups. Credentials and the formal definition of occupations play a role here. This works well for explaining individual-level outcomes. Wright claims that except in the study of education, income, and wealth, this micro approach works better than macro ones of a more Weberian or Marxist kind. The Durkheimians are good on lifestyles, tastes, and political or social attitudes.[21]

A key to Weberian theories is *opportunity hoarding* or social closure, by such means as credentialing, licensing, the color bar, or gender exclusions. One could even see labor unions as a form of opportunity hoarding from the point of view of precarious workers, an idea I'll come back to. Perhaps the most important mechanism of opportunity hoarding is private property itself. Wright: "The core class division within both Weberian and Marxian traditions of sociology between capitalists and workers can therefore be understood as reflecting a specific form of opportunity hoarding enforced by the legal rules of property rights."[22]

Both Marx and Weber saw property as fundamental to a relational concept of class. Both grasped the distinction between objectively defined class and subjectively lived class. Both thought humans followed material interest in the long run. Marx shared Weber's view that status groups impeded the effects of the market and constitute an alternative basis of collective action. Both thought the rationalization of market relations would abolish status groups over time. However, Weber was much less inclined to think classes would polarize and become the key social dynamic.

The Weberian theoretical frame sees class as relational but downplays the Marxist concept of *antagonistic* classes. For Marx, ruling classes extract a surplus from subordinated classes. They may do so through domination, through exercising power and coercion, as in the case of the slave mode of commodity production in the American South. They may do so through exploitation, through the extraction of the value of the activity of a subordinate class, as in the case of the liberal capitalism in Great Britain during Marx's time. One might even ask if there have been additional means of class antagonism invented in our time.

Class in Weber is more closely connected to the theme of *rationalization*.[23] Rational forms of power supersede nonrational forms of power such as honor or patriarchal authority. Marx thought this rationalization simplified class, whereas Weber did not. Weber thought class determined life chances within rationalized society. He was less interested in deprivation than in instrumental rationality. Marx was more interested in class exploitation in production; Weber in class as factor in determining life chances in the market. Wright: "Marxist class analysis includes the Weberian causal processes, but adds to them a causal structure within production itself."[24]

Class is thus part of rationalization, part of the abolition of the traditional peasantry, part of the transition from landed aristocracy to agricultural landlords. Class is part of the rise of the calculation of material interest. The peasant, who owes a duty to the baron, becomes the farmer who pays rent to the landlord. The slave, who is the property of the plantation master, becomes the sharecropper, formally "free" but in debt to the landlord, as often as not the old master in a new role. "While class per se may be a relatively secondary theme in Weber's sociology, it is, nevertheless, intimately linked to one of his most pervasive theoretical preoccupations—rationalization."[25]

My question here would be: why would one think, if this has already given rise to more than one kind of rationalization of class antagonism that overlapped and interfered with each other, that it would not give rise to another? The farmer–landlord antagonism arose out of the antagonism between serfs and the nobility.[26] Serfs lost their lands by force or debt and fled to the cities, while a rationalization of agricultural production led to the expansion of a surplus that might feed urban populations, who would become urban workers, in an antagonistic relation to capitalists. And yet landlords and capitalists also had interests that contradicted each other. But did rationalization stop, with the creation of classes of farmer and worker? What happens when the production, not of food or products, but of new information itself becomes rationalized?

Weber did not have a lot to say about labor, but where he did, it was in terms of work discipline. Employers are free to hire and fire. Workers lack ownership, but workers are responsible for their own social reproduction. These are the conditions under which *indirect compulsion* operates. But it raises the problem of how to get maximum labor effort. Wright: "running throughout Weber's work is the view that rationalization has perverse effects that systematically threaten human dignity and welfare."[27]

But Weber does not integrate interest in labor discipline and domination into the category of class. Here we need a bit of Marx, for whom, as Wright says, "exploitation infuses class analysis with a specific kind of normative concern."[28] Exploitation steers research to questions of class as relational in *both* exchange and production. "Weber's treatment of work effort as primarily a problem of economic rationality directs class analysis towards a set of normative concerns centered above all on the interests of capitalists: efficiency and rationalization."[29]

Wright's synthesis of Marx and Weber makes exploitation fundamental even as it makes particular use of the idea of opportunity hoarding as that which defines the "middle class." From there one could build up a picture of the United States as highly polarized by exploitation, a country where middle class opportunity hoarding is being eroded by what he calls *neoliberalism* and *deindustrialization*. I think this can be understood more clearly in terms of new forces of production that instrumentalize and rationalize information, giving rise to new property forms and hence new class relations, including an antagonistic relation between a hacker class tasked with making novelty out of information (the condition of it becoming property) and a vectoralist class that owns or controls the vector of information control and domination itself.

The separation of the vectoralist–hacker class antagonism from the capitalist–worker antagonism emerges out of the development of the forces of production, which generated an extensive and intensive rationalization—or better yet, *abstraction*—of the production of information. As Adorno and Horkheimer pointed out in their own synthesis of Marx and Weber, the rationalization of means serves irrational ends, not least in treating nature as a mere thing to be exploited in the same manner as the working class is exploited, through the subordination of everything to the commodity form.[30] Each successive form of class rule may be more abstract than those it subsumes, but it isn't more rational.

The antagonism internal to the vectoralist–hacker class relation has all three components of a class relation: property, authority, and expertise. It emerges in the first instance out of a rationalization of so-called intellectual property law, which increasingly encloses information in something close to a private property right. Vectoralist domination over all subordinate classes is sustained by the automation of relations of authority, which take the form of pervasive surveillance and quantification—a rationalization of all aspects of human activity.

Domination through expertise turns out to be an interesting and subtle question. The rise of the vectoralist class changes the kinds of credentials that appear to have value for class power. These became increasingly technical in nature. Access to such qualifications appears to offer the possibility of class mobility. Here the perspectives of Weber and Durkheim are useful supplements. Opportunity hoarding through control of access to elite credentials sustains social closure and the exercise of occupational power through expertise. Since both men and women, not to mention women of color, sometimes have elite credentials in the formal sense, their exclusion ends up being enforced by more old-fashioned means of authority and domination, through the "toxic work environment."

A lot more could be said about that. Here I simply add the possibility of an additional axis of class antagonism, in addition to property, authority, and expertise. This is what we might call the *technical dimension* of class antagonism, where it is built into the form of the information vector itself. This has many aspects, from the design of algorithms determining credit to the development of object-oriented programming environments, which allow for the rationalization of the production of component parts of programming by a dispersed and disempowered hacker class while preserving central control of proprietary code. Rather than domination or exploitation, this form of class antagonism emerges out of asymmetries of information and protocols of selective access and control.[31] Forms not only of class but also of gendered and racialized discrimination have migrated from relations of property, authority, and expertise and have been encoded as technical (or algorithmic) forms of power.[32]

Thinking about class antagonism today might then require two steps. For the first, we are indebted to Wright: Durkheim's interest in the moves of the game and Weber's interest in the rules of the game can be folded into Marx's larger perspective, on the changing of the game itself. But for the second step, we are on our own: in the absence of faith in the leap into a gamespace without domination and exploitation, we have to reimagine the possibilities of action for subordinate classes. Wright speaks in very measured terms of the normative aspect of Marx's project. He does not name the trope toward which its heliotropism tends: Communism. But his analysis of class rests nonetheless on it as a "hidden god."[33] Wright maintains the faith in the absence rather than the presence of possibility in either its revolutionary or reformist forms.

I think we might have to reimagine the normative goal itself, based on the combined experiences of the farmer, worker, and hacker as subordinate classes. What is the just means of making and distributing matter, energy, *and* information? That might then inform strategies and tactics for changing the vectoralist game. But in the meantime, we might have to make do with struggles over the rules of the existing gamespace and over the everyday lives of players, hustlers, and grinders making their moves, as the vulgar blues language of the times—from hip hop to trap—would have it.[34] Besides reaching out to those indebted to more classical approaches of Durkheim and Weber, Wright addresses prominent contemporary social theorists who try to offer original perspectives. Here I'll take sides with Wright against some of the most widely known alternative social theories—Thomas Piketty, Guy Standing, and Wolfgang Streek—while introducing their perspectives into the thought experiment that this is no longer capitalism but something worse.

Thomas Piketty deserves credit for putting inequality back on the agenda as more than a mere problem of unequal opportunity.[35] His empirical work shows that the sharp rise in income of the top 10% is really that of the 1% or even the .1%. A fair bit of this came from the rise of super salaries rather than income on capital. The CEO "class" is setting its own pay. Here I would want to inquire as to how, in a political economy running on information, the capacity to control (but not exactly own) the means of production accrues to a class that presents itself as the celebrities of information control itself. Commanding attention becomes a form of class power.

The technicalities of Piketty's work centers on the capital:income ratio as a way of measuring the value of capital relative to total income of economy. As Wright says, "Piketty's basic argument is that this ratio is the structural basis for the distribution of income between owners of capital and labor: all other things being equal, for a given return on capital, the higher this ratio, the higher the proportion of national income going to wealth holders."[36] As growth declines, the capital:income ratio rises. There's a rise in the weight of inherited wealth, while concentrations of income also rise. It's the worst of both worlds: a rentier "class" plus a CEO "class" of appearance-peddlers carving up the world between them at the expense of everyone else.

Picketty starts out with a class analysis but loses it once he gets into the empirical work, where he treats CEO income as return on labor, as most income tables do. Wright: "In the modern corporation many of the powers-of-capital are held by top executives.... They occupy what I have called contradictory locations within class relations ... They exercise their capitalist-derived power within the class relations of the firm to appropriate part of the corporation's profits for their personal accounts."[37]

But is their power really "capitalist-derived," or is it now something else? Something like a joint managing of appearances between those who represent a firm to the market and the market that is supposed to value it. But how to value a company when so much of its asset base takes the form of information? A corporation today is among other things a brand, a slew of patents, a logistical process, a corral of expert hackers turning out new intellectual property. How can information be turned into value, and an opportunity to be hoarded, when there aren't really private languages, and information is in principle a nonrivalrous good?[38]

Piketty does not separate out real estate from capital, yet there might be good reasons to do so. Landlords and capitalists are already different kinds of ruling classes with overlapping but not identical interests. Ground rent and profit are not the same kinds of surplus extraction. Landlords, perversely, may benefit from the rise of the vector in ways Capital does not. As Matteo Pasquinelli says, today's landlords (often with giant global property portfolios) increase their rents by extracting the information value that the presence of the hacker class produces.[39] On the one hand, attracting so-called creatives or techies to a neighborhood drives out working class and non-white tenants. On the other hand, the new residents add layers of information to the place that can be recuperated as value to sell it to bankers and lawyers and drive out mere hacker class tenants in turn. Gentrification is but a step to aristofication. One could think further here about Ricardo's ancient tension between ground rent and profit, but with the focus shifted from the rural to the urban and the monopoly rents to be extracted from urban locations.[40]

Guy Standing is the name most associated with the now widely discussed idea of the *precariat* as a class rather than just a bad life chance.[41] He offers a three-dimensional definition of class, as structured by relations of production, relations of distribution, and (interestingly) relations to the state. He identifies seven classes: plutocracy, salariat, proficians (professional + technician), working class, precariat, unemployed, and lumpen-precariat. The precariat have insecure jobs. Their sources of income other than wages are disappearing. They become less citizens of the state and more like mere denizens. Not only are their jobs precarious, they are vulnerable within relations of distribution and marginal to the state.

The precariat includes people bumped out of working class communities and families who experience a relative deprivation in relation to a real or imagined past. It also includes migrants and asylum seekers for whom the present is absent. The precariat increasingly includes people falling out of an educated middle class—think academic adjunct labor—who lack a future. For Standing this makes a potentially "dangerous class."

Marxists might think of the precariat as workers who (in Weberian terms) experienced poor life chances. Standing thinks there are antagonisms between the precariat and the working class. But do the precariat and workers have distinct interests? Maybe not.[42] Maybe they can share an interest in changing the game (although one might want to say more here about how workers and the precariat might have different interests about the rules and moves of the game). Unionization, for example, can secure some sort of steady work for the workers in the union, but whether it benefits those outside of it is an open question.

Wolfgang Streeck argues, in a Durkheimian vein, that capitalism works better when there are constraints on rational, self-interested action, based on trust, legitimacy, and responsibility.[43] The wrinkle Wright introduces is to argue that the level of constraint on self-interest that is optimal for capitalists is below that which is optimal for workers. Capital seeks to remove constraints to augment its power even past the point where these are economically inefficient.

Wright: "The zeal to dismantle the regulatory machinery of capitalism since the early 1980s was driven by a desire to undermine the conditions for empowerment of interests opposed to those of capitalists—even if doing so meant under-regulating capitalism from the point of view of long-term needs of capital accumulation."[44] One could see this a bit differently by separating out the interests of the capitalist and vectoralist class. The regulatory regime emerging in the last quarter century favors the mobility of information, and not just finance, as a means of coordinating economic activity transnationally, at the expense not just of workers but of those forms of capitalist enterprise tied to physical plant and infrastructure, and thus with an interest in local, regional, or national relations of trust, legitimacy, and responsibility.

We can read Wright's conclusion against the grain: "Enlightenment of the capitalist class to their long-term interests in a strong civic culture of obligation and trust is not enough; the balance of power also needs to be changed. And since this shift in balance of power will be costly to those in privileged positions, it will only occur through a process of mobilization and struggle."[45] What if those capitalists tied to actually producing things in a particular place already know this, but they have lost power to a quite different kind of ruling class, which operates at a higher level of abstraction, or in Weberian terms, at a new stage of rationalization? They own or control the information about things, rather than the things themselves. This is not inherently more rational, but it is more abstract, and hence more powerful.

To imagine new kinds of class compromise might require a rethink about which classes could compromise. Since there appears to be no way to change the game, Wright looks to those who wanted to change the rules within the game, such as Walter Korpi and Gøsta Esping-Anderson, Scandinavian social democratic inheritors of Ernst Wigforss.[46] But one has to ask if it's possible to revive social democratic strategies from the era of the great national manufacturing industries in an era where the information vector greatly lowers the cost of geographic dispersal and puts the old capitalist manufacturing firms and regions in direct competition with each other on a global scale.

Wright advocates for some salutary counterhegemonic strategies, based in geographic rootedness, local public goods, and worker's cooperatives. But one has to wonder whether such things are all that viable (at least as traditionally conceived), given that the forces of production drive increasingly abstract relations of production, which appear then as transnational legal and treaty forms protecting information as private property. Trebor Scholz proposes a form of *platform cooperativism* as a more contemporary approach.[47] The vectoralist stack needs to be countered with a counterstack on the infrastructural level.

Wright: "Changes in technology may make the anchoring of capitalist production in locally rooted, high productivity small and medium size enterprises more feasible."[48] One might call this the Brooklyn-effect, after the boom in small business, even manufacturing, there.[49] But while the actual products have some connection to locality, such localism relies on an information infrastructure or vector stack owned and controlled by the vectoralist class: Google, Amazon, Paypal, and so forth all get their cut. Their power may take the form of a vectoral infrastructure that enables them to extract information asymmetries from both capital and from subordinate classes and to accumulate asymmetric information about all of these activities now subordinated to the vector.

Thus, where Wright says, "I assume that an exit from capitalism is not an option in the present historical period,"[50] I think we have to question that assumption, but not in a good way. Maybe this is already not capitalism, but something worse. It's not just a rentier bubble of speculation spooling out of the "real economy."[51] One could no longer know in advance which part of it is real at all—and perhaps one never could. This is an era not just of so-called neoliberalism's "aggressive affirmation and enforcement of private property rights"[52] but of the creation of new forms of private property and new antagonistic relations over it, particularly in the form of intellectual property.

There's a lot to be said for the way Wright subsumes rival social theories as collaborators within the larger frame of a fairly traditional Marxist sociology. But perhaps that in turn has to be put back in contact with a more vulgar attention to the transformation of the forces of production, and in particular how information emerges as both a technical and social force. One could then, as a further step, bring this perspective together with the study of the *metabolic rift*, wherein the instrumentalizing of information mobilizes the whole planet as a rationalized sphere of resource extraction under the sign of exchange value.[53] To the point where this abstraction of the vector becomes completely irrational, threatening to take the whole planet down with it.

Maybe we need an *asocial science* that rethinks whether one can even conceive of the social as a separate domain of analysis at all. On the one side, the social meshes seamlessly with information technology; on the other, it depends on planetary scale resource mobilization causing catastrophic metabolic rifts. One might be in need of an even "bigger" conceptual framework within which to rest Wright's partial synthesis as a component part (a question I'll return to in Chapter 6).

One might think again also about the kinds of social forms and tactics of class existence. Particular groups of workers and hackers now have to negotiate a far more temporary sense of employment existence. The vector is nothing if not a platform for making all human activity interchangeable and replaceable. Here Wright's signature concept of *contradictory class locations* can be thought on both its intended structural level and as a good guide to understanding everyday experience.

An example, as Angela McRobbie has observed, is working class women who will try to work in the fashion industry despite low pay, long hours, and precarious employment because they don't want jobs, they want to be creative.[54] They want to be hackers, not workers. Whole industries now function on the promise of creative activity and effect a bait and switch. The real job is labor, often even manual work, and for women in particular often affective labor, where the job is really just keeping clients happy.

Something similar happens in the tech industry in so-called start-up culture. It employs hackers in the narrower, more Durkheimian sense of the word, people who code. (Even here, a lot of it may turn out to be labor in the sense of repetition and the filling-in of software-generated forms already created and designed and indeed owned by someone else.) The promise, however, is that the hacker can become the owner. The bait and switch is the lure of becoming part of the ruling class. The risks of enterprise are disproportionately shifted onto the hacker while the rewards disproportionately return to that fraction of the vectoralist class known as venture capital. Some parts of the hacker class are offered a possible escape into the vectoralist class at the price of increased precarity that rarely comes to pass. Most find themselves constrained by routines that turn them more into wage labor.

People working in fields that are "creative" or "tech" live with Durkheimian senses of "class" as a constant. Everything is about groups defining collective identities in all sorts of slippery ways. A less common topic is a Weberian one about opportunity hoarding. There are constant eruptions of anger and attention to inequalities derived from access to credentials, for example. Or we could attend to how sexual harassment drives women off the path in particular workplaces, or how certain industries systematically exclude people of color. These are important conversations and indeed issues to fight.[55]

What's less common is to think this within a larger concept of class. Class has Wright's three dimension (property, authority, expertise) and now a fourth: the power of *information asymmetry*. Race and gender oppression now connect to all four dimensions of class. The immediate problem is that the other ways of thinking class categorize people into clusters. They are indeed things that the vector of information technology can track and manage. It can tell you how many women earn how much money, or how many employees report being something other than white. Class in the Marxist sense is harder to make palpable.

First, class means class *antagonism*. It's not a category, it's a relation. One that sometimes connects not individuals but what Gerald Raunig and others call *dividuals*, units of being smaller than an individual.[56] It turns out that individuals can indeed be further divided. One could think of class locations as including contradictory ones if one thinks of the people located by class as individuals. Or you could think of classes as quite neatly creating locations for dividuals, which don't always correspond to the individuals of which they are parts. In this manner, the tension people feel about parts of their existence, as worker and hacker, or hacker and aspirational vectoralist (and so on), can be made sense of another way.

Second, if class locates dividuals rather than individuals, it's no surprise that the way people think about their experience of class if often conflicted. What I would call *vectoral culture* encourages everyone to imagine that they are entrepreneurs of the self, playing the stakes of their own animal spirits in the great casino of life.[57] Twenty years of hip-hop lyrics have articulated a sophisticated range of thoughts and feeling about what that's like. One's public self is supposed to be a hard-charging boss. As Cardi B. raps, "I'm a boss you a worker bitch."[58] What it means to be a boss is now modeled on the vectorialist rather than the capitalist class. It's about accumulating asymmetric relations of information. It is about commanding and monopolizing attention. It's about monetizing appearances. The thing to aspire to own is a brand, starting with the branded self and branching out from there.

If this is the public face the subaltern has to adopt, whether worker or hacker, the private feelings it masks may be something else altogether. Failure to live up to your own personal brand is understood through languages that are medical, therapeutic, or "spiritual."[59] This is a world of boredom, anxiety, depression, lack of focus, lack of will. It can take a lot of pharmaceutical management—legal and illegal—to produce the public face of today.[60] To the extent that there is a language about power that can address these experiences, it negotiates perspectives from critical race theory and feminism, as it should, but often stops short of a language of class. That language, against which these others struggled to find room, has atrophied as vectoral power has subsumed capitalist power as its subordinate form. The language of class analysis (in the Marxist sense) appears outdated, because it is. It no longer includes all the classes in contention. If we think synchronically about a matrix of antagonistic classes that includes emerging ones, then capitalism can be returned to *historical* thought from its holiday in eternity.

5

A Time Machine Theory of History

> We no longer know what socialism is,
> or how to get there,
> and yet it remains the goal.
>
> —Deng Xiaoping

Let's say you have a time machine. Let's say you take it back in time to the mid-seventies. You hop out and look about for some influential people of that time. You explain to them a few things about what is going on in the twenty-first century. Some of your stories make sense to some of them; other stories sound completely nuts.[1]

For example, let's say your time machine sent you to mid-seventies China. You explain that, by the second decade of the next century, the fate of the global market will be in the hands of the Chinese Communist Party. That would sound pretty crazy. The mid-to-late seventies in China saw the fall of the Gang of Four, the Maoism-lite of Hua Guofeng, and then finally Deng Xiaoping coming to power in the late seventies. But even by then, the China of today would still seem unimaginable to everyone—except Deng Xiaoping.[2]

If you took a time machine back to the Soviet Union in the mid-seventies, you might find a more mixed reaction. Leonid Brezhnev is in his second decade in power, which looks like it will go on forever. The proxy wars aren't going too badly, with a good showing in Angola and a decisive win in Vietnam—at least until the Soviet invasion of Afghanistan in 1979. You'd probably come across some ideologues who think it's all going fine and you must be mad to think it will be over by the start of the nineties. On the other hand, the economy is just lumbering along. Productivity is flat. The military consumes a huge slice of resources. Vladimir Putin, who joined the KGB in 1975, might already be thinking about a way to stay on the power-track without having to really believe in this particular kind of power.[3]

If you took the time machine back to the United States in the mid-seventies, you might be the one who is confused. Jimmy Carter is President. New York is broke and broken. Microsoft has just been founded. If you tell the think tank "intellectuals" of that era that the Soviet Union will collapse, you might also have gotten a mixed reaction there, too. Let's not forget that the ancestors of today's neoconservatives were pretty certain it couldn't happen. The Soviet Union was not just a regular repressive state to them. It was a *totalitarian* one, which had wormed its way so far into every aspect of everyday life that it could not be brought down by internal forces, but only by jabs from without—by arming Islamic militants to fight it in Afghanistan, for example.[4]

But if you told the neoliberals, they would get it.[5] They said all along that planning won't work because it's just too clunky a way to organize the *information* in an economy, and information is what economies are all about. But those guys did not have a lot of influence back then. Their time had not quite come.[6] And when they talked about information, they really only meant markets. They would not have known any more than anyone else why the founding of Microsoft would turn out to be a big deal. (Later they will pretend they did.)

It is a commonplace to think of the Soviet Union as dead and buried and of the People's Republic of China as somehow becoming just like the West in everything except politics. There are other perspectives. One is that far from being a thing of the past, "Communism" is alive and well and still in charge of a fair chunk of the planet. What the hundred million strong Chinese Communist Party rules over is something a bit less like the "neoliberal West" and a bit more like what the Soviet Union might have been had it stayed the course and stuck with the New Economic Policy, which lasted from 1921 to 1928. Incidentally, Deng Xiaoping was in Moscow briefly during that period. One wonders if he was thinking quietly to himself about something like the New Economic Policy version of "socialism" for fifty years before he got to build it and watch it run off.[7]

The specter haunting Europe, haunting much of the world, is the specter of anti-communism.[8] It might be a useful perspective to imagine that it was not just the Soviet Union that died; its corresponding other half, the so-called Free World, might also have died with it.[9] Of course, it wasn't all that free, if you include all the beatings, the torture, the murder, and the massacre perpetrated by the US military and its proxies around the world: Suharto in Indonesia, Pinochet in Chile, Mobutu in the Congo, and the Shah of Iran—those thugs and butchers were part of the "free" world too.[10] And in the United States itself, the state's response to Black Liberation was to embark on mass incarceration.[11] But on the other hand, one small contributing factor to the partial success of social democracy and civil rights in the West was the need to compete for loyalty with international communism, which at least laid claim to a narrative of universal justice and the final victory in History of a higher form of life.

Even Communism's enemies had to admit this was a pretty compelling story. There was feudalism, now there's capitalism and alongside it socialism, which evolves into Communism, where history ends.

"We will bury you," as Khrushchev said in 1956, when people still took what Soviet leaders said seriously.[12] The most celebrated minds in the West did their best to come up with mythic-epic-poetic grand narratives that could be as compelling, but where the Free World got to be the future rather than the past.[13] A surprising number of them were rather lapsed Marxists and socialists: James Burnham and the managerial revolution; Daniel Bell and the postindustrial society; Walt Rostow's stages of growth and takeoff theory; Alvin Toffler's future shock.[14]

Most of these theories avoided thinking about class conflict. In that respect they looked back to Saint-Simon rather than Marx.[15] They were stories about technology and progress—or in today's terms, acceleration.[16] Actually, Marxists beat them to accelerationism, too. This part of the story is rather neglected by all sides. If there was an original accelerationist, it was J. D. Bernal, whom we met in Chapter 3. A prominent British scientist of the interwar years, he wrote a dazzling accelerationist tract called *The World, The Flesh and the Devil* (1929), which envisioned the consummation of rationality and desire not so much as making human life better, but of transforming the human into some sort of posthuman species-being.[17]

He was also aware it could all go horribly wrong. Bernal: "Scientific corporations might well become independent states and be enabled to undertake their largest experiments without consulting the outside world... The world might, in fact, be transformed into a human zoo, a zoo so intelligently managed that its inhabitants are not aware that they are there merely for the purposes of observation and experiment."[18] As one sees, he was starting to have some inkling of where the forces of production might lead and what kinds of ruling classes might control them.

Bernal converted to the Communist cause shortly after, and together with the left wing of the Social Relations of Science movement, thought a bit more coherently about science and technology as transforming the forces of production. For Bernal, the transformative capacities of science put scientific workers—one prototype for what I would call the hacker class—on an opposing path to Capital, which restricts the full force of technological change to that which is compatible with the profit motive. As early as 1939 Bernal thought a scientific and technological revolution was under way that was qualitatively different from the forces of production developed in industrial capitalism.[19] That had been piecemeal and accidental; this was intentional and planned. That was based on a rudimentary know-how; this was based on controlling matter, energy, and information understood through abstract, conceptual, and ever-evolving knowledge.

Bernal was an enormously influential figure in his prime—which was roughly from 1930 to 1950.[20] His application of scientific knowledge to the problems of war made the D-Day invasion possible. He was a pioneer on the question of the organization of scientific information. He was made a Fellow of the Royal Society for his x-ray crystallography. But his loyalty to the Soviet Union doomed his career once the wartime alliance broke up and the Cold War was on. Still, the Social Relations of Science movement (whose left wing he represented) helped politicize scientific and technical workers around the world, from Denmark to Japan.[21]

Ironically, given that he stuck with the Soviet Union even after it invaded Czechoslovakia in 1968, his idea of the scientific and technical revolution was alive and kicking in the intellectual ferment of the Prague Spring, which had tried to come up with a "socialism with a human face." The phrase is attributed to Radovan Richta, who put together the book *Civilization at the Crossroads*.[22] Published in 1966, it is another lost accelerationist classic. It quietly argued that Soviet style socialism had failed but that the state ownership of the means of production should make possible a new kind of socialization, not just of labor and its product, but of the totality of knowledge.

When I went shopping online for this forgotten book, I ended up buying what had once been Daniel Bell's personal copy. It is not hard to see the accelerationist theories of the Free World, such as Bell's, as responding not just to classic Marxist historical prophecy, but also to what was still a very real fear up until the '70s: that the East rather than the West would figure out how to turn the scientific and technical revolution into a new mode of production. But in neither the East nor the West had accelerationist thinkers quite grasped the strange ontological properties of information and how information science, even more than the science of matter and energy, would end up being the distinctive feature of the next century.[23] But at least the Marxist accelerationists had almost grasped one important feature of the world to come: namely, that it would be a world with new kinds of class antagonism.

It is ironic that the Soviet Union failed to build the Internet; the Soviets went at it like Americans, whereas the Americans succeeded because they went about it like Soviets. What would become the Internet was the product of the state investing in basic research in fairly big, collaborative labs, just as Bernal had said it should happen. If we have to come up with a one-word explanation of the failure of the Soviet version, we might settle on "competition."[24]

The war had given the American state the habit of funding collaborative research projects involving both basic science and engineering, and with a surprising amount of sharing of ideas rather than keeping discoveries secret with an eye on monopolizing the patent. The basic, shared knowledge about computation, communication, radar, and electrical engineering emerging out of wartime was the foundation for the Pentagon's substantial investment in all these fields during the Cold War.[25]

Bernal was a bit too much of an orthodox Marxist to wrap his head around information theoretically, but he got it as a practical problem.[26] The kind of physics he did was not about understanding smaller and smaller particles, which is what we think of as the main line of modern physics. It was about understanding bigger and bigger ones. How do atoms come together not just in molecules, but in giant, organic macro-molecules? Advances in the techniques of x-ray crystallography made it possible to answer such questions. This was the path that would lead others to understanding the structure of things like vitamin B12 and insulin (for which his student Dorothy Crowfoot Hodgkin won the Nobel prize).[27] These techniques also contributed to Watson and Crick's famous work on DNA (with an uncredited assist from Rosalind Franklin).[28] All this would end up requiring fantastically complex computation, and Bernal was one of the first to bring more or less modern computing into this field.

In short, for better and worse, computation enables operations to be performed on what would now be called "big data."[29] That makes possible the simulation of really complex things, like organic molecules or even whole economies. Some had even thought that Soviet-style socialism could be made to work if prices were made variable and computation introduced into resource allocation decisions. But the powers that be nixed it. They didn't want to give up command of their command economy.[30]

Radovan Richta must have known that Soviet cybernetics had failed to shift the Soviet mode of production on from dysfunctional state socialist control.[31] There's a hint in his book that this was something of a class conflict: the scientific workers versus the party apparatchiks. But with a few notable exceptions, the former were still insiders, not willing to test the patience of a state that had jailed, tortured, and killed so many of their predecessors.[32]

The most notorious example of Soviet abuse of science was the Lysenko affair.[33] Trofim Lysenko was the son of a peasant and an agronomist whose essentially Lamarkian view of evolution became official policy, at the expense of those scientists who followed Mendel's discoveries in genetics. But this well-known case of state interference in science in the East obscures certain things about power and science in the West. For one thing, western ideologues exploited the Lysenko case for propaganda purposes with little regard for the complexity of the facts. Their call for "freedom" in science seems to have meant "free" as in Free World. Science was coopted into secret military programs. Scientists who raised difficult questions about the politics of science lost their visas, their security clearance, even their laboratories and livelihood.[34]

The most absurd case was surely that of Tsien Hsue-Shen, a Chinese immigrant to America. In the postwar period he had settled into a top-notch career in the new field of rocketry (renamed "jet propulsion" at Caltech, to make it sound more respectable). But it seems he had unwittingly socialized with people who were in the Communist Party. So he was deported—to what had since become Communist China. There this formerly apolitical scientist became both a loyal Communist and the architect of the Chinese missile program. The Silkworm tactical missile, descendant of his designs, was even used in the complicated proxy wars of our own times against US forces.[35]

But this was nothing compared to the general demobilization and demoralization of the scientific left in the postwar years. Progressive scientists such as Bernal were under attack, as were the unions that had grown to express and unify the interests and aspirations of scientific and technical workers. Ironically, big science really was now a creature of massive state support as Bernal had predicted, but the ideology of science made to prevail was not Bernalism, but an image of science as a "market of ideas" cooked up by his ideological nemesis Michael Polanyi.[36]

Those whose prejudice is to think that science must be inherently reactionary or apolitical or an extrusion of mere "metaphysics" would do well to study just how much coercion and co-option it took to blunt the power of progressive and leftist science in the West after the war. Polanyi's group was even the beneficiary of what we now know to have been a CIA front, the Congress for Cultural Freedom.[37] If you went back in time to the seventies and told an ailing Bernal that by the early twenty-first century there would be left-Heideggerians, it might have caused him another stroke.[38]

And so here we are then, trying to understand what happened over the course of the second half of the twentieth century, equipped with critical theories detached from their former connection to the political struggles in the sciences and hobbled by Cold War injuries that still go largely unexamined.[39] No wonder then that there are few good conceptual tools for understanding how the forces of production really were revolutionized in the period following the war. We have instead descendants of the consensus theories in the spirit of Saint-Simon.[40] For instance, the "ecomodernists" insist that there's nothing that can't be solved by yet more technology in its current form, steered by the wisdom of today's ruling class. The line of thought initiated by Bernal, which in a particular vulgar Marxist style understood historical change on the basis of a thorough knowledge of the forces of production as riven by class conflict, has been much less prominent.

The field was left vacant in the postwar years for one body of theory that really did have a bit of a clue about information: neo-liberalism.[41] It did not really have its day in the sun until it was apparent that the Soviet Union was not a clear and present danger. Caught between the oil shocks of the early seventies and relentless working class militancy amid flat productivity growth, the idea took hold among the ruling classes of some leading western nations that it was time for an actual class war against labor rather than simulated nuclear war against the Soviet Union. Indeed, one might wonder whether nuclear détente between the United States and the Soviet Union came out of a mutual interest in suppressing working class discontent within those empire's respective home worlds.

Neoliberal policy was not universally adopted, but that too was part of the problem. If you could go back in time to the mid-seventies and you explained to people that by the early twenty-first century the Japanese economy would be in stasis, and some of its once powerful companies up for sale, your predictions would have been greeted with some surprise—back in the seventies it was Japan that was the threat to American economic dominance. Japan seemed to have figured out how to contain class struggle within a dynamic that raised productivity. And it had figured out how to incorporate the information workers possess about the production process into the quality control of industrial manufacturing. In Japan, state and corporations worked together to limit the free market domestically and combine economic resources for an all-out drive to conquer export markets.[42]

Back during the war, Japan never attacked continental America with its Zero fighter-planes. The best it could manage was dropping a couple of incendiary bombs from unmanned hot air balloons made of rice paper glued together by schoolgirls and carried across the Pacific on the jet stream.[43] Rather than Zeroes, Japan eventually invaded the United States with Mitsubishi Colts and Galants—cars that incidentally were made by the same conglomerate as those Zeroes. So with the Soviet and Chinese geopolitical threat contained—the latter with Nixon's "ping-pong diplomacy" of the seventies—the challenge was more of the order of working class militancy on the one hand and sophisticated Japanese exports on the other. The neoliberal attack on labor, in the name of "free" markets as the most efficient processors of information, got under way.

Another anomaly in relation to the story of the rise of neoliberalism is Italy. By the mid-'70s it seemed to be in the throes of some sort of spectral civil war. The Red Brigades were kidnapping people. The secret police seemed to be running the state. The Communist Party was close to a "historic compromise" that would put it in power, in partnership with its old nemesis the Christian Democrats. This had spawned a dissenting Autonomist left movement and corresponding theory. The secret police were doing their best to jail, exile, or silence those theorists, such as Antonio Negri and Paolo Virno. But it looked like Italy really could swing left.[44]

If you were to go back in time and explain to Italians living in the mid-seventies how culture industry tycoon Silvio Berlusconi came to power in the nineties, they might not be amused.[45] In the seventies, major corporations such as Fiat and Olivetti had tried using cheap labor from the rural south, but many of those young workers became politicized.[46] So instead they tried automation as a way to control the power of labor. Either way, Italy like Japan was not on the neoliberal path in the postwar years, even if (unlike Japan) it was not particularly successful at conjuring up an alternative. Italian exceptionalism did give rise to a vigorous strand of Marxist theory, but one more rooted than it might want to acknowledge in eccentric local conditions.[47]

The myth of neoliberalism is that the *idea* of neoliberalism came first, and then politicians like Margaret Thatcher and Ronald Reagan made it policy and then law. This narrative is sometimes popular among leftists despite its clearly idealist view of history.[48] I think it's possible to tell the story another way. After all, what made it possible to implement neoliberal policies in the first place? What changed since the seventies that made it possible to globalize banking and build vast international supply chains to combine components of a manufacturing process from all over the world?

The clue is already there in the stray fact that Microsoft came into existence in the mid-seventies. It was not information as an idea —free markets—that changed the mode of production. It was a vast, global infrastructure in which information enabled the control of flows of money, machines, resources, and labor. If you can use a computer to calculate the positions of ten thousand atoms in a protein, you can use it to calculate a global production system that routes around the power of militant labor in a factory in Detroit.[49]

There isn't really a time machine that will take you back to the seventies. Or rather, we have only a one-way time machine, or perhaps not a time machine so much as a *tome* machine. You can look in the archive for some neglected storylines, and the past comes back as something else. Maybe something even more amazing than the surprises you could spring on people in the past if you had a time machine are the surprises the past can spring on us through the tome machine of the archive. Maybe we could practice a kind of historical art, of telling the stories otherwise, as a way of inquiring into why certain kinds of story are neglected or suppressed. The default stories selected from the combinatory of story elements may be arbitrary narrative habits.

Here's a story, then: It is an error to call our times *neoliberal* when its politics are not "neo" and its politics are not "liberal," anyway. The politics of the present might just as well be described with the equally retro term *alt-fascist*.[50] It is all about securing ruling class power through the manipulation of racial and ethnic prejudice and the use of surveillance and overt violence to suppress dissent. It is centrally about the prison–industrial complex, expanded now on a global scale, as Angela Davis reminds us.[51] What is new is not the politics at all, which is a farcical double of the superstructures of old, but rather the mode of production underneath it. Here one might say that the economics are not "liberal" either and that is what makes them new. Forces of production organized around information change the commodity form.

It is a strange thing, this mode of production. What Bernal and Richta called the *scientific and technological revolution* really did happen, and in the West, not the East. But it was the product of a weird kind of "socialism." It came out of a wartime socialization of scientific and technical power. Scientists and engineers, in academic and corporate laboratories, cooperated with each other. Their innovations weren't immediately patented, they were shared. That laid the groundwork for postwar developments in the forces of production. To some extent this "socialism" continued, under the auspices of the Pentagon's Advanced Projects Research Agency, which among other things funded key work in computation.[52]

If there was a key innovation that came out of this strange western state-socialist military–industrial complex, it was the technics of information. It took a while for the pieces to come together. By the early twenty-first century, the odd thing is that the state-socialist sponsored scientific and technical effort, made first to defeat the Axis powers and then to defeat the Soviets, ended up being a way to compete with Japanese industry abroad and to defeat the working classes at home. A basically socialized research program became the means to build an infrastructure—what Benjamin Bratton calls *the stack*, what I call the *vector*—for a systematic and global privatization of objects, subjects, and the information in between them.[53]

That this was not an inevitable destiny of science and technology was masked by the suppression of critical and dissenting voices among scientists themselves. Bernalism, or the Social Relations of Science movement more broadly, was shut down in the red scare politics of the Cold War. In the relative absence of that strand of thinking, the available stories for accounting for this historical period have lacked a sense of the class conflicts internal to these new forces of production and the extent to which they were likely to transform capitalism, such as it was in the late twentieth century, into something else.

The story that is best known about science and technology during the war is the Manhattan project and the atom bomb. But perhaps it was not the only piece of the puzzle that mattered. The war in the Pacific was probably the biggest logistical operation ever conducted up until that time. Robert McNamara, who would later run the Ford Motor Company and then the Pentagon, was an apprentice logistics expert during the war. These were pioneering efforts to control the movement and combination of incredibly complex arrays of resources across vast territories using communication and computation.[54]

What started out as the means to beat the Axis powers, and then contain the Soviets, and then to compete with Japanese industry, was in the end the means to globalize production, exploit the newly available cheap labor of the People's Republic of China, and destroy the power of organized labor within Italy, the United States, and throughout much of the overdeveloped world. But there's a paradox attendant to this. Capital thought it was using some new kinds of communication and computational power in its struggle with labor, but in the end the capitalist class too ended up being subsumed under that power. The capitalist class became a subsidiary ruling class to the *vectoralist class*. Capital is dead; the Vector lives.

A capitalist class owns the means of production, the means of organizing labor. A vectoralist class owns the means of organizing the means of production. The vector has a double form: the form of vector along which information is to be routed (the extensive vector), and the form of the vector along which information can be stored and computed (the intensive vector). A vectoralist class also owns and controls the production process through patents, copyrights, brands, trademarks, proprietary logistical processes, and the like.

It is curious that if one looks at the world's biggest corporations these days, a lot of their power and property is in vectoral form. Many of them don't actually make the things they sell. They control the production process by owning and controlling the information. Even when they do still make the stuff, a quite remarkable amount of the valuation of the company comes from portfolios of intellectual property, or proprietary data about their customers, and so on. Capital was subsumed under a more abstract form of technical power.

When considering the vectoralist class, then, three further points suggest themselves. First, it seems to be able to extract value not just from labor but from what Tiziana Terranova calls *free labor*.[55] Even when you just stroll down the street, the phone in your purse or pocket is reporting data back to some vectoralist entity. The vectoralist class seems to be able to extract revenue out of qualitative information in much the same way as banks extract it out of quantitative information. Perhaps the exercise of power through control of quantitative and qualitative information is characteristic of the same ruling class.

Second, the vectoralist class subordinates the old kind of ruling class, a capitalist class, in the same way that capitalists subordinated the old landlord class that subjected rural production to commodification through ground rent. In that sense, the rise of a vectoralist class is a similar and subsequent development within intra-ruling class dynamics. The vectoralist class still sits atop a pyramid of exploited labor, but it depends also on extracting a surplus out of another, fairly privileged but still subordinate class.

I call it the *hacker class*. Bernal already had an inkling of this development when he tried to articulate the interests of scientific workers in and against capitalism, but this was not quite the hacker class yet. That had to wait for the development of sophisticated forms of intellectual property, which are in turn embedded in the design of the interface for the creative process. This transforms the qualitative work of producing new forms of information in the world into property that can be rendered equivalent in the market. In short, a new class dynamic, between vectoralist and hacker, was added to an already complex pattern of relations between dominant and subordinate classes.

Third, the political economy of the former West rather than the former East was the one that was able to develop the implications of the scientific and technical revolution, in the form of the rise of the vectoralist class. But it was the state form of the former East that has prevailed in the former West. The vector is not just a means of transforming production. It is also a way of transforming state power.[56] Data can be collected for the purposes of a logistics of economic control; data can also be collected to run the surveillance and security apparatus of the state. The western states too had their surveillance apparatus, but it was never as total as those of the East. The new model worldwide uses the vector to realize the dreams of the KGB of old, an information state. This is what Guy Debord called the stage of the *integrated spectacle*, combining the worst of the former East and West.[57]

The West is now the former West. Its economy became something else. It isn't capitalism any more—it's worse. It takes even more control away from work life and everyday life. It expands the exploitation of nature to possible extinction. It is certainly not the wonderful dream of a "postindustrial society," still less Bernal and Richta's accelerationist socialism. It is a relatively new and more elaborate form of class domination, one in more or less "peaceful coexistence" with the Russian former East, whose global significance is reduced to that of predatory oligarchy monopolizing a resource export economy.[58] The Soviet Union paid a high price for not figuring out the role of information and reaching a modus vivendi with its scientific workers.

Both now co-exist with the People's Republic of China, which under Deng Xiaoping followed something more akin to the Japanese rather than the so-called neoliberal model, of suppressing wages and funneling the surplus into export-led growth. Whatever forces may have been pushing in a more neoliberal direction in China seem to have been decisively defeated after the 2008 financial crash. Xi Jinping consolidated his power and set China on a different course. Perhaps the neoliberal state is not the only model of the information state. China is attempting another kind. An authoritarian information state, no doubt, but the states of the former West are hardly in much of a position to criticize given their own tendencies.

In the West, vectoral power has so routed the working class and driven down its wages that it can no longer consume what China manufactures. Its ability to do so was propped up temporarily by debt. But now the whole system is awash in bad debt and surplus productive capacity. Sensing a crisis of overproduction looming, the Chinese Communist Party directed its matrix of state and corporate actors to embark on an extraordinary plan to restart the silk road and open new markets for its manufacturers across central Asia and beyond. The dominant idea still seems to be, as it was under Deng, to expand the forces of production, this time beyond the borders of China itself—and this time allied to control of the vector.[59]

In its own mind, the legitimacy of Communist Party rule rests on its capacity to both accelerate the infrastructure and manage the consequences for the superstructure of this social engineering project as it pushes outwards beyond the borders of the People's Republic of China.[60] That this was to be the destiny of a Leninist party is so inconceivable to either the western left or right that both seem to pretend that this monstrous project is not really happening. What would require considerably more thought would be to figure out what is distinctive and what is generic in the intraruling class politics that make China's ambitious alignment of state, vector, and capital possible.[61]

Benjamin Bratton thinks that what he calls the *stack*, or what I call the *vector*, generates a distinctive kind of geopolitics, one in which the former sovereign states have to negotiate with a kind of power based in distributed information infrastructures, producing a relatively novel kind of virtual geography.[62] He would have us attend not just to China's strategic competition with the United States, but also to what he calls the "First Sino-Google war of 2009."[63] The vectoralist class in the former West seems to be detaching itself from the space of the representative state and investing in transnational vectors. Meanwhile, China's ruling class is building something different, in which state territory and stack territory coincide.

Of all the trips in our imaginary time machine or actual tome machine, those back and forth to the People's Republic of China are surely the most perplexing, at least for those of us from the former West, and possibly those from the former Soviet East as well. It is particularly difficult for western Marxists. There is still a hardy band of bearded old professors and votaries of various sects who think they keep alive the flame of an "orthodox" Marxism—some of them even extinct flavors of westernized Maoism. This is a strange conceit when seen from the point of view of the existence of the hundred-million-member Communist Party of China. While one might want to dissent strongly from their version of it, orthodox Marxism today is really whatever that party says it is. One's heretical version might best take the thorough critique of "Xi Jinping Thought" as its point of departure now, rather than the ancient quarrels dormant in dead tomes.

To someone from the former West, the willful "ultrabolshevism" of Chinese Marxism is a curious thing, particularly once it became the mythic combinatory through which the now ruling party narrates and justifies its own trajectory to itself.[64] In the former West, it is common to imagine, and not without a shade of Eurocentrism, that we are the custodians of what Marxism is, so the ruling party in China must just ignore it or pay lip service to it or invoke it purely hypocritically. There may indeed be elements of that.

The Communist Party of China does not really care what those of us from the former West think Marxism is. To them, whatever it is, its fate is determined in China, not the former West and certainly not in the former East. And its fate was to become the mythic generator of narratives through which a Chinese adaptation of the Bolshevik Party narrates its own history to itself. This is hardly a cynical exercise, as the party's grip on power depends in some small part on the cogency of that story.

The party drew three very different kinds of story from the Marxist combinatory at three junctures in its history. Mao Zedong thought emphasized class struggle as a voluntarist activity, putting politics in command, forcibly making a working class agency out of a mostly peasant population led by the party.[65] Deng Xiaoping thought shifted instead to the development of the forces of production to accelerate industrialization and the formation of some kind of capitalist class, led by the party.[66] Xi Jinping thought shifts again to the ambition of China's leadership of world history, through the building of a massive infrastructure of the vector or stack kind that drives global trade and supply chains that route around those of the former West, led by the party.[67]

Mao had warned about capitalist roaders, but he knew nothing of the vectoralist silk-roaders to come after them. Capital in the former West broke the power of labor by using the information vector to coordinate a new global geography of production, and in particular by moving actual production to China, where a capitalist class emerged under the auspices of the party. That class might indeed have subsumed the party entirely. It is quite possible that the richest billionaires on the planet are Chinese Communist Party grandees and their families.

The Chinese state might well have taken a "neoliberal" turn. However, with the collapse of the global financial system in 2008, triggered by speculative madness in the US mortgage-backed securities market, China seems to have decisively changed tack. The Chinese state and economy, like others, are increasingly driven by a plurality of forms of big data vector rather than exclusively by finance. The ambition of the Chinese ruling class seems to be the control of a transnational value chain more through ownership and control of the vector of information than through ownership and control of the means of production. Factories outsourced from the former West to China are being outsourced again to even less developed states (including some in the former East) through Chinese-controlled information and logistics infrastructure. The party now seems to view itself as an agent of world history, realizing a global universality—but with Chinese characteristics.[68]

There is not enough world out of which to build China's ambitious global vector or anyone else's. The intensive vector of computation can now model just about anything, from complex biochemical forms to whole economies to the whole biosphere. And as it turns out, that biosphere is in trouble. The scientific and technical revolution at one and the same time pushes the biosphere to crisis point and yet also yields the only reliable information we have about climate change and other symptoms of the Anthropocene.[69] Once more, there is a moment in which the scientifically trained start to ask questions about the system within which their knowledge is being exploited. Only this time it's not poison gas or nuclear weapons or DDT, it's the whole process of vectoral and commodified production and consumption that is called into question, which has become more and more abstract and less and less rational.

If you were to go back to the seventies and explain to climate scientists that by the early twenty-first century, climate change caused by industrial production has been definitively shown to raise global average temperatures, they would probably want to closely study the models and the data you have brought back with you to show them, but they would probably not be surprised at all. However, they would probably ask you what people in our time are doing about it. And you will wish they hadn't asked.

6

Nature as Extrapolation and Inertia

> it is some nature to conjure with amidst
> the fry up formally unfurled as progress
> —Drew Milne

Ours is an era in which startlingly powerful forces of production are ripping the planet to pieces at a faster rate than ever before, but the very same technology driving the disaster is also the basis of sophisticated ways of knowing the extent of the damage. This is Cassandra with augmented reality, and it leads to all sorts of ugly feelings.[1] The problem of what *nature* might be returns from exile among the hippies. For a long time, it seemed like a critical gesture to insist that reality is socially constructed. Now it seems timely to insist that the social is reality constructed.[2]

This pessimism can quickly flip into panic, dread, resignation, or cynicism. It seems that the destruction of natural conditions of existence is an inbuilt feature of how commodified modes of production have always worked, starting with the earliest colonial exploitation projects.[3] Exchange value subordinates any other value to its own reproduction.[4] If this is all imagined to be capitalism, then it becomes pressingly urgent that it be superseded by another mode of production, one without its *exterminist* drive.[5] And yet Capital appears in this conception to be eternal; it changes only in appearances. The possibility of its negation appears ever more remote.

The sixties were perhaps the last years in which the negation of capitalism by an external revolution even seemed possible. Capitalism in the overdeveloped world and imperialism in the underdeveloped world looked for a moment as if they could be overturned by a new kind of proletarian militancy and a new kind of anti-colonial movement, respectively.[6] These external revolutions did not come to pass. Both Marxism and postcolonial theory retreated into their genteel phase.[7] If the capitalist-imperialist base was to march on for eternity, then perhaps there were ways to turn the cultural or political superstructures against it.

Take the tome machine back to the world of French philosophers of the seventies, and you can find an alternative way of thinking about collective action in history forged as a response to this impasse. Rather than *negate* capitalism, was it possible to *accelerate* it? Perhaps its own internal revolution would lead to its demise. It was an idea that had occurred before, but accelerationists do not usually stop to look back. The new wave of acceleration began with Deleuze and Guattari's book, *Anti-Oedipus* (1972), and in its most charmingly delirious form, Jean-François Lyotard's *Libidinal Economy* (1974).[8] It took a right-accelerationist turn in the writings of Nick Land, collected in the book *Fanged Noumena* (2011). I offered a left-accelerationist version in *A Hacker Manifesto* (2004).[9]

Here is the accelerationist theme from *A Hacker Manifesto*: "A double spooks the world, the double of abstraction. As private property advances from land to capital to information, property itself becomes more abstract. Capital as property frees land from its spatial fixity. Information as property frees capital from its fixity in a particular object. This abstraction of property makes property itself something amenable to accelerated innovation—and conflict. Class conflict fragments, but creeps into any and every relation that becomes a relation of property. With the emergence of a hacker class, the rate at which new abstractions are produced accelerates. Where private property dominates, as in the vectoral world, it accelerates the hack by recognizing it as private property, but thereby channels the hack into the relentless reproduction of the commodity form."[10]

"Third nature becomes the environment within which the production of second nature accelerates and intensifies, becoming global in its apprehension of itself. The containment of free productivity within the representation of property, as managed by the state in the interests of the ruling class, may accelerate development for a time, but inevitably retards and distorts it in the end. Far from being the perfect form for all time, property is always contingent and awaits the exceeding of its fetters by some fresh hack. The past weighs like insomnia upon the consciousness of the present."[11]

"There are two directions in politics, both of which can be found in the class struggle within nations and the imperial struggle between nations. One direction is the politics of the envelope, or the membrane. It seeks to shelter within an imagined past. It seeks to use national borders as a new wall, a screen behind which unlikely alliances might protect their existing interests in the name of a glorious past. Deleuze: 'Their method is to oppose movement.' The politics it opposes is the politics of the vector. This other politics seeks to accelerate toward an unknown future. It seeks to use international flows of information, trade or activism as the eclectic means for struggling for new sources of wealth or liberty that overcomes the limitations imposed by national or communal envelopes."[12]

What I think of as a *centrist accelerationism* emerged later in Nick Srnicek and Alex Williams's *Inventing the Future*.[13] This ably but unconsciously restates some of the themes of J. D. Bernal about the expansion of the forces of production, as one might have found them through his influence on British Labour leader Harold Wilson.[14] This is from Wilson's famous 1963 speech: "In all our plans for the future, we are re-defining and we are re-stating our Socialism in terms of the scientific revolution. But that revolution cannot become a reality unless we are prepared to make far-reaching changes in economic and social attitudes that permeate our whole system of society. The Britain that is going to be forged in the white heat of this revolution will be no place for restrictive practices or for outdated methods on either side of industry."[15] In their version, Wilson's white heat of technology might not only overcome scarcity but, in an original twist, abolish work itself.[16] It's a theme they develop from the Italian autonomist Marxists. The more centrist flavor comes from their hostility to what they call "folk politics" which is local, small scale, horizontal, connected to affect and identity.

All these species of accelerationism have a glaring omission. None of them has much to say about the Anthropocene, although I did attempt a self-criticism along these lines in *Gamer Theory*.[17] It's ironic that schools of thought with wonderfully vulgar enthusiasms for technology and science don't pay attention to that leading science of our time: climate science. Here some of the negationists appear at least to be actually paying attention. But there the common tendency is to make eternal capitalism into even a geological epoch: the "Capitalocene."[18]

This just returns us to the enervating spirit of the times. Nowhere does it appear that there is a movement of the subordinate classes with the power to negate Capital. And even if there was, the negation of Capital is not in itself a solution to the problem of feeding seven billion people (and rising) without crashing the planet. This is before we even get to the genteel hubris of thinking one can tell earth scientists what to call a geological period.

What accelerationist and negationist Marxism have in common is that they conceive of history as *social* history. They are not vulgar in the sense of the earthy. Both make a prior cut between the human and the nonhuman and concern themselves mostly with the former. What we need is another axis, a "spatial" rather than a temporal one. It's the question of how to think both the continuities and partitions between nature and culture, or what Donna Haraway calls *nature-culture*.[19] Revisiting this axis seems timely, given that one thing the Anthropocene might imply is that there's no taking for granted that there is any separation between natural history and social history. Let's get back in the tome machine and find some texts that will bring us forward into this perspective.

At one end of this "spatial" axis, let's place Joseph Needham. In *Time: The Refreshing River* he developed the concept of *extrapolation*.[20] Although Needham had read Marx in German in the twenties, he was more influenced by Ernst Mach's insistence on limiting the role of theoretical speculation.[21] He did not become a Marxist until Nicolai Bukharin led a delegation of Soviet scientists and science historians to London in 1931.[22] Needham's radicalism had just as much to do with attempting to synthesize two consequences of the English revolution: the egalitarian communalism of the Levellers and the science in the service of social improvement of the Invisible College, which later evolved into the Royal Society.[23] The forces of production accelerated by the efforts of the latter would in the end overcome their atomistic worldview and create the conditions to realize the social and political project of the former.

Needham was a biologist, his field of study being embryology.[24] How does a tiny clump of undifferentiated cells grow into the form of a particular species of organism? Besides its material and experimental challenges, this was a research line with conceptual questions, particularly about form. Like Marx, Needham was a reader of Lucretius, from whom he took the image of a small number of discrete types of atom, but put the stress on the bonds that assemble them together into an array of forms.[25] He abandoned the Aristotelian concept of a higher power or final form that drew the elements together into itself —the root of most *vitalist* and new materialist theories which want to add a special extra principle to explain the difference between the living and the nonliving.

Needham resisted this superadded vitalism but ran up against the limits of mechanical metaphors and chemical theories for accounting for the development of embryos. Instead, he borrowed (détourned) the image of the *field*.[26] In a field theory, development is determined by proximity effects. The form and function of the part depends on relations with adjacent parts; patterns of adjacency shape the whole. Crystals are an example of such field adjacency from the nonorganic realm. But rather than a reduction of biology to physics, this implied the introduction into physics of a problem from biology, the problem of how proximity in a field causes certain kinds of forms to assemble. The high degree of organization in organic systems stem from fundamental properties of physical matter. But matter has organizing activity at scales beyond the atom and the molecule.

The autonomy of biology as a science had to do with the scale of organization it studies. The unity of science derives from articulating the relation between the study of different scales of organization rather than from the sovereignty of physics. This was not a kind of reductionism, nor was it a general systems theory, applicable universally. The question of form has to be studied in its specificity at each scale. The biochemistry Needham was engaged with provides an understanding of how molecules can align in patterns and structures, which can fold and twist into a larger scale of much more diverse forms.

Needham moved on from the study of embryos to the study of

technological development in China that began with the first volume of his *Science and Civilization in China*, a project that continued for the rest of his long life.[27] He took a similar approach to the relation between the social-technical and the biological as he did to biological and the physical. Just as there is no magical vitalist spirit that differentiates biology from physics, there is no special principle of the social, either. Yet this is not a reductionism. Just as the biological is the study of forms specific to a given level of organization, so too are the social sciences. And just as biology brings its own question to physics, social science brings its own question to the natural sciences. What forms are possible? The biological (and geological) set a limit on the range of possible forms, but they do not mandate that the existing ones are necessary or eternal.

It may be possible to *extrapolate* from both natural and social-technical history a range of other possible forms. The more strictly atomistic worldview central to the western moment in scientific development typified by the Royal Society had in Needham's view run its course. He thought that because of China's long history of complex social organization, which enabled a rich legacy of field-based worldviews, and because of its revolutionary turn in modern times, that China was in a position to extrapolate from both natural and social history the next stage in the organization of knowledge and social-technical form.[28] If only one could go back in a time machine and ask his views on the rather different version of such a vision being implemented by Xi Jinping.

Needham's extrapolation might be one pole of an axis of thinking natureculture as an affirmative theory and experimental practice. But what is at the other end of this axis? Let's call this *inertia*. If Needham thought affirmatively about what forms the natural world might suggest for the social, *inertialists* think it negatively. Nature as the not-social other. They attend to what resists social action. They think the historical movement, whether it be in the form of negation or acceleration, as rising up only to fall down again, accreting back into dead matter. Perhaps the most significant thinkers of inertia are, or could be, Jean-Paul Sartre and Maurice Merleau-Ponty.

Lucien Goldman once offered the provocative thesis that Martin Heidegger's *Being and Time* (1927) was basically a response to Georg Lukács's *History and Class Consciousness* (1923) but shifted into a strictly philosophical realm. Both were attempting to think outside of dualism in a manner that preserves the honor of philosophy as having sovereignty over a totality. For Heidegger there is a lost and prior whole before the separation of object from subject; for Lukács there is an historical agency—the party of the working class—that can become the unitary subject–object of history. In one, the good totality is lost; in the other, it is to come. What stands in the path of recovering the thought of Heidegger's lost whole is the *inauthentic*; what stands in the way of the consciousness of a totality to be made in Lukács is *reification*, of which commodity fetishism is just one instance.

Beginning the story of inertia here helps account for the strange way that Sartre turned a reading of Heidegger toward a kind of inside-out Lukácisan dialectic of the totality. This was how he moved around the combinatory from negation to inertia. As is well known, Sartre's reading of Heidegger is a highly "creative" one, a *détournement*. Sartre produces not an ontology of being but a phenomenology of the human condition, his famous *Being and Nothingness*.[29] If for Heidegger the inauthentic masks a basic unity, for Sartre, it becomes a terrible chasm. Nothingness is all there is at the heart of being. The subject confronts the object as something irredeemably foreign. After Hegel, he calls the object the *in-itself*; he calls the subject the *for-itself*. The for-itself is defined negatively. There's no affirmative statement of an anthropology here, no species being of the order of Feuerbach or the young Marx.[30]

The conscious human subject, the for-itself, is not an identity. It is nothing but a difference, a lack. The for-itself depends on its desire for what it is not. The lack that the for-itself feels can never be overcome, as there is no prior unity to uncover, nor is there a final form to posit as a goal at the end of History in the manner of the negationists. Nor are the in-itself and the for-itself in any relation of reciprocity. The for-itself lacks the in-itself, but not vice versa.[31]

It is not Capital but unhappy consciousness that is a permanent condition. Sartre's thought (at this time) is relentlessly individualist. Relations between atomistic subjects are conflictual. Only the objectifying gaze of an external, third-party observer can make squabbling individuals cohere into a group by producing a sense of community, the *us-object*. But this has its limits. There's no God who can occupy that place for the whole species-being. Nor is there ever a time of reconciliation. The for-itself is future-oriented, and the future is always open, a realm of freedom.[32]

Sartre agrees with Lukács contra Engels (and his vulgar Marxist followers such as Needham) that nature is undialectical, but for Sartre history cannot be thought separately from nature. In Sartre, nondialectical nature permeates the human, in the form of the body, troubling the for-itself. *Nausea* (also the title of Sartre's first novel) reveals the body to consciousness.[33] As Martin Jay remarks in *Marxism and Totality*: "In short, the radical heterogeneity between history and nature that was posited by Hegelian Marxists like Lukács and Kojève in order to save dialectical totalization for human practice was interiorized within the realm of human history itself by Sartre."[34]

We are confronted by the *facticity* of an alien world that is not for us. And yet we must act, and we are responsible for all our acts: we are condemned to freedom. And yet we dwell in *bad faith*, refusing to accept that we are our choices. What we must do is choose a *project* and embark on it. The goal of such projects is however an impossible one: the fusion of the for-itself with the in-itself. There is no God to fuse with, just the inert, repulsive facticity of an alien nature. And so as Sartre says in *Being and Nothingness*, "man is a useless passion."[35] Such was the worldview Sartre formed in the 1930s, a depressing and dark time, where it would have been foolish to expect any reconciliation of reason and History.

Then came the war. The Resistance raised the question of *commitment*.[36] We are free to make our lives and are defined by our actions. We suffer anguish at having to choose.[37] Our actions cannot be gratuitous, as in the Surrealists or Bataille, but at the same time Sartre starts to see constraints on the projects through which freedom is realized. Already, in the margins of *Being and Nothingness*, was the category of *situation*, that indistinct zone where the contours between the in-itself and what the for-itself might be able to realize are not known in advance. The Situationists will later expand that thought into a whole practice, not of the free act, but of the *constructed situation* in which different acts are possible.[38]

It was probably Merleau-Ponty who pushed Sartre toward Marxism. For Merleau-Ponty, we are condemned not to freedom, but to meaning. Our consciousness is embedded in both the body and the social. The Resistance for him meant not Sartrean freedom, but the ambiguities of History. The Resistance was a collective intervention in History, not an individual project, but nor was it Lukács's party as unified object-subject of History negating the reified world to bring into being the true totality. In his *Adventures of the Dialectic*, Merleau-Ponty saw historical undertakings as adventures without rational guarantees and stressed the experimental character of Marxism. He defends revolutionary terror (a line of thought repeated in Žižek).[39] Collective action cannot choose its situation. The proletariat still remains the transcendent figure of hope.

Merleau-Ponty came to realize that politics can't really articulate itself to the totality. As he writes in *Adventures*: "The Marxism of the young Marx as well as the 'Western' Marxism of 1923 lacked a means of expressing the *inertia* of the infrastructures, the resistance of economic and *even natural conditions*, and the swallowing up of 'personal relationships' in 'things.' History as they described it lacked density and allowed its meanings to appear too soon. They had to learn the slowness of mediations."[40]

Inertia, infrastructure, mediation—against which negation has no magic power. There is no leap out of the mundane, vulgar matters that confront action in a recalcitrant world. This was the brute experience of the early Soviet Union of which Andrei Platonov wrote so well.[41] The negationists lack a sense of history's intractable institutional quality, of the residues and detritus within which any attempted collective action has to summon the energy to come into being. Merleau-Ponty: "Marx was able to have and to transmit the illusion of a negation realized in history and in its 'matter' only by making the non-capitalistic future an absolute Other. But we who have witnessed a Marxist revolution well know that revolutionary society has its weight, its positivity, and that it is therefore not the absolute Other."[42]

Merleau-Ponty accused Sartre of *ultra-bolshevism*, of still entertaining the myth of the party as transcendent subject–object of History, bringing reason into History. Sartre, he says, does not get the web of symbols, the passivity of subjects, the intractability of objects. If one source of Sartre's grappling with Marx was Merleau-Ponty, the other, strangely enough, was Heidegger. In the "Letter on Humanism," Heidegger contends that Marx had at least posed the problem of alienation and extracted from it a conception of history that found a real material basis for that estrangement in capitalist relations of production of modern technological forces of production.[43]

Sartre was still resistant to totality as a category and thus also to the terrorist practice of liquidating particularity in the name of History. He was not yet thinking alienation historically, only phenomenologically, and had no way to respond to the leading historical thought of the time. Given the violence with which the "orthodox" Marxists of the time attacked him, Sartre's disinterest in such a move is quite understandable. Still, he was a fellow-traveler of the party from 1950 to 1956 and did his best to do the party's thinking for it.

All of which comes to a head in Sartre's *Critique of Dialectical Reason* (1960).[44] Sartre still stresses the primacy of the individual and the resistance of lived experience to any abstract system. He thinks totality as a dead exteriority produced by human action. What Lukács called *totality*, and the young Sartre called the *in-itself*, this later Sartre calls the *practico-inert*. It is that great heap of worked over matter that resists our actions and shapes them to its habitual patterns, rather like the way Marx thinks of fixed capital as dead labor over and against living labor in the "Fragment on Machines" and elsewhere. The practico-inert is irreducibly other, even though produced by collective human labor. It is in a way a complete vulgarity.

The for-itself is now thought as *praxis*, as self-definition through action in the world. But does all action lead to the practico-inert? Unlike in Lukács, there is no affirmative model of the unalienated at the end of History, because for Sartre the for-itself is always negatively defined, by its lack. Our species-being is nothing but lack, desire, project. Praxis can however be a kind of *totalization*—a term borrowed from Lefebvre—which is dynamic, living, and above all unstable.[45] Sartre thinks a rational total history is possible but only as a futurity, a project for praxis to posit. He does not quite want to give up all faith in History. But he is nervous about History as the last court of appeal, as in Lukács, and is well aware of the tendency to make the ends—History—justify any means to the party. History cannot replace God as the objectifying gaze.

In any case, most of the time what we experience is repetitive. Any totalization via praxis is ephemeral. There is a sort of anti-dialectic of *passivity*. Praxis can happen as the act of a *fused-group*, coming together to realize a project, but they all fall back toward the practico-inert. Indeed, the praxis of a fused group may just contribute to the practico-inert some new layer of detritus, some new sources of inertia. The fused-group falls away back into what he calls *seriality*. The world is not really knowable through collective praxis. Group solidarity might be the result of coercion as much as of freedom. True acts of reciprocity, of fusion and praxis, are very rare even if in Sartre there is no magical void from whence such events might emanate.[46]

In the *Critique*, Sartre translates the terms of *Being and Nothingness* into a new language: the *inauthentic* becomes *seriality*, *project* becomes *praxis*, and *facticity* becomes *scarcity*. The initial structure of the world is one of scarcity, to be negated and overcome by human need. The negativity of need or desire organizes the scarcity of the in-itself into a situation. The useless passion that is man makes the world over in a project with meaning. This is the *negation of the negation*: the negativity that is human need organizes the negativity that is scarcity. Scarcity is the reason History is a world of violence.

This is an almost Hobbesean world, except that in Sartre it is not human nature that is violent, it is the situation. Our species-being is simply negativity and lack, which becomes violent in the situation of scarcity, preventing reciprocity with others. Scarcity transformed by human desire, a negation of a negation, is the project in its collective form, a praxis, and is also a totalization, which means an organized activity toward a goal. Praxis organizes the heterogeneity of the world into a coherent situation toward an always deferred goal.

Sartre preserves the radical difference separating the human and nonhuman of *Being and Nothingness*. Consciousness is alienated from itself in things and also in other people. These initial dualisms are the elements on which Sartre builds an integrated view of History. As in Marx, so in Sartre: being is not reducible to thought; thought is integral to the world in the form of activity. We make our own history, but not in situations of our own choosing.[47] Sartre now pays closer attention to the unchosen nature of these situations, which are themselves the result of past human history-makings. Marx wrote at the beginnings of the capitalist mode of production proper, when "all that is solid melts into air."[48] Sartre writes at the point where it becomes "late" capitalism, where all that capital dissolved into air calcifies again into rigidities of one kind or another. Praxis does not confront natural situations in Sartre, but rather the already worked-over results of previous projects. In a way, he was already talking about the Anthropocene.

The rough, rotting, decaying detritus of failed projects—which in Platonov fall outside of meaning—appear in Sartre as a kind of anti-dialectic, a counter-finality conjoined with the finalities of praxis. This anti-dialectic is what produces the *practico-inert*—objects that are not just objects, but objects in which the residues of the human are mixed. Projects are not only circumscribed by scarcity, but also by a layer of the practico-inert that precedes them and renders the project null in the end. This is Hegel's *cunning of reason* in reverse, an undoing and abrading into insignificance of any accelerationist desires, no matter how rational. The cunning of reason, working through History, is no match for idiomatic matter.

It is not just the world that fills up with the practico-inert as the residue of failed praxis. The human becomes thinglike and passive in order to impart something human into the passivity of the thing. Here Sartre generalizes Marx's heretical concept of fixed capital as form containing dead labor as content. Just as in Marx, where labor–commodity are two sides of the same thing, in Sartre it is praxis–worked-matter. Worked-matter shapes activity, and the subjectivity that results is *seriality*, which is a side-by-side anonymity and indifference—like those moments when a homeless person begs for change on the subway and everyone just pretends they are not being addressed by this other person's entreaties.

In seriality, "everyone is the same as the Others in so far as he is Other than himself."[49] The center of my world is not in me, it is in other people for me—and the same for them. We all ignore the beggar on the subway, as if she or he is not addressing us. In seriality, everyone stands in exteriority to each other. Examples of seriality for Sartre include the market and broadcast media, although it is hard not to see today's social media as pure seriality, too. Seriality happens everywhere from the means of production to the memes of production.[50]

To seriality, Sartre counterposes the *fused group*. This might seem like playing a "folk politics" off against some kind of claim for a "rationality" of planning. Sartre thinks the fused-group as the emergence of an event that produces a subjectivity.[51] The fused-group produces not more things but an authentic subjectivity. In the fused-group, everyone is the center, and otherness becomes identity. The fused-group is no longer a dualism of my indifference to you and vice versa.

In the group we are united by the threat of an external third, interiorizing the threat to sustain the group. Each becomes a third to all the others. This was certainly how it felt during the folk politics of Occupy Wall Street. It seemed like we were a tiny fused group to the extent that there was constant fear of being displaced or confronted by the cops. But even that was not enough, in the long run, to sustain it, and it melted away, a useless passion.[52]

The fused-group is temporary and something of an illusion. Belonging is defined by its nonexistent totality. At this stage everyone is a leader. Apparent leaders are really only the mouthpieces for the desires of the group. The group is oriented to a futurity, to an appointment with a future time. The means through which fused-groups impose themselves on History are not pretty. Sartre's two examples are the French and Russian revolutions, which in some ways betray the same pattern. Here we can note in passing that, unlike Needham, Sartre's worldview remained preoccupied with what we might now think of as the former-East and the former-West.

In both revolutions, the fused-group binds itself to a future appointment with History by a blood oath. Constituent power pledges itself to its group desire and comes into being out of the negativity in this act. The pledge could be to liberty, equality, and fraternity; or it could be to peace, land, and bread. But the pledge sets up the conditions for identifying the traitor and the group-structure in which the terror appears to sustain the impossible totality of the fused-group.[53]

There is then a bracing pessimism to Sartre, and not just concerning the fate of negation as a revolutionary project. Subjectivity is either passively shaped into the same form as the practico-inert, or it fuses into groups that have no being, that collapse back, or worse—which impose themselves on History through terror. As such, *Critique of Dialectical Reason* is a profound response to Stalinism. But I think it's more than that. It is as if he was already describing the Anthropocene as we now feel it, where objects are already worked-over by past praxis into a practio-inert and force us into relations of seriality and passivity.

Inertia provides a way of thinking about how the struggles of the hacker class came together for a moment, not so much in a fused group as in clusters of human and inhuman cyborg actors plugged in to the project of technical acceleration as liberation. But it collapsed into seriality, which the vector now reproduces in a new form—the seriality of social media, which is just the consumer-end experience of whole chains of interactions with the same serial form.

Interestingly, in *Search for a Method*, Sartre says that "Marxism, while rejecting organicism, lacks weapons against it."[54] It is not clear whether Needham's organicism is the sort of thing he had in mind, but it certainly appears enabling for thinking the four quadrants of the combinatory of historical thought at the moment: an acceleration —negation axis, and an inertia—extrapolation axis. Acceleration and negation actually share an optimism about a purely social totality that can be rationalized; extrapolation and inertia reject this and insist that the opacity of the social-technical world results in part from its imbrication in nonhuman life or in dead matter, respectively. What negation and inertia have in common is the labor of the negative, while extrapolation and acceleration share an affirmative approach to the making of History.

In the Anthropocene, the key tension is not between acceleration and negation, but between acceleration and inertia. Inertia is what acceleration has to acknowledge and overcome as the already-existing critique of its Promethean projects.[55] One path to that overcoming lies through the theory and practice of extrapolation from organicist understandings of forms of organization that traverse the presumption of a nature–culture divide. Organicism might deal instead with what Donna Haraway calls *naturecultures*, which are attentive not just to the conceptual but also technical means by which what Karan Barad calls the *cut* is made, and out of which an artifact of "nature" appears in a rationalizable form, separated out from its cultural, social, and technical conditions of existence.[56]

The very variety and complexity of its forms ought to rule out any neat ideological insistence as to what nature it is that we're supposed to follow. Inertia insists on that kernel of nature that is resistant to thought and which, far from being a world of external objects, is part of our very existence. The nonhuman is within the human. Out of a praxis, in and against the practico-inert, might come not so much the fused group as something more like the *constructed situation*.[57] If some aspect of the inert world is a part of the human; some aspect of past praxis is also a part of the nonhuman practico-inert. Praxis is a matter neither of the human folk politics of fused groups or of the nonhuman seriality of planning but rather the inhuman construction of situations that are muddled hybrids of both.

Extrapolation attends to the natural world but is at the same time critical of received ideas as to what nature is or could be. This is the quickest answer to the recurring problem, borne of the received ideas of a genteel Marxism, that whenever one even dares mention nature, one has committed the original sin of Malthusianism, in which the invocation of nature as limit necessarily becomes a defense of existing hierarchies and enforced scarcities.[58]

Extrapolation need not treat science as sovereign. For instance, Drew Milne writes poems about lichens: "a fungus and a photosynthetic / symbiont in stable vegetative / structure being body specific / the cell walls discovering in / mutual agriculture an extreme / for deserts to a tune of many."[59] It's part of a series called "Lichen for Marxists" that extrapolate a language worthy of Francis Ponge for an earthy endurance in part from a close observation of this other nonhuman life.[60] These poetic observances spawn a détourned manifesto.

Drew Milne: "We, the Biotariat, hold no human truths to be self-evident, acknowledging rather that all humans are mutually dependent on unacknowledged life forms, that they are endowed by their genealogy with certain heavy responsibilities, that among these are the Biosphere, the Solar Commune and the mutual furtherance of Peaceful Symbiosis. That to secure these responsibilities, alliances are assembled among humans, deriving their lasting vitality not just from human wills but from the continuation of all species. That whenever any form of Corporation becomes destructive of these ends, it is the duty of the people to alter or to liquidate it, and to institute new formations and alliances, laying its prospects on such principles and organizing its powers in such forms as to the best of their Scientific Understanding shall seem most likely to effect their safety and happiness. Sustainability, indeed, requires that Corporations long established should not be changed for light and transient causes; and accordingly all experience hath shewn, that humans are more disposed to suffer, while Global Warming appears inevitable, than to take up arms against the forces to which they are accustomed. But when a long slick of Industrial Pollution and Technological Innovation, pursuing invariably the same Profit Motif, evinces a design to bring them unto species extinction, it is their responsibility, it is their duty, to throw off such Corporations, and to provide new regulative frameworks for future Symbiosis."[61]

If we could time-machine this text back to Needham, it might have appealed to him, as a reader of Marx, of organic form and of a certain generous tradition in English poetry. Meanwhile, Sartre had already moved away from the categories of Capital confronted in History by the force that would negate it and raise up from it the Communism imminent to its unfolding. In its place, he tried to think *praxis* and *scarcity*, where scarcity is a negativity that praxis in turn negates. It's a way of thinking what no mode of production has resolved. Scarcity predates Capital and endures beyond it. The project to overcome it can (and must) be freely chosen but can never close the gap between the human and the nonhuman worlds. At best it might result in an inhuman apparatus less worse, less damaging, than the last.

Sartre's is an atheist theory. There's no God (no third) who can mediate one desire's negation of another, who can release subjects from their indeterminacy, their freedom. But note that an a-theist theory, one without God, still has Him there in negative, as an absence. It's not so easy to finally have done with His judgment.[62] In the same way, it's not so easy to have done with Communism, or what in Cold War terminology was called The God That Failed.[63] It is either weakly present or not present, but the fixed idea of Capital is still tied to it as the only conceivable negation.

In the same way as one is an atheist, maybe it's time to be an *acommunist* (always lower case). This is not capitalism, it's worse. We're free to desire another project for what might come after capitalism. It won't be Communism; as it turns out, the exit from Capital through external revolution was an off-ramp not taken. God is dead; Communism is dead. It is, at best, the legacy code of the Chinese ruling class. But that does not exhaust the imaginal faculty of the subordinate classes, whose vulgar energies may even in this practico-inert world have some surprises in store.

7

Four Cheers for Vulgarity!!!!

> the removal of the elevated point of view,
> which adds immeasurably to the *number* of things
> and their names
>
> —Pier Paolo Pasolini

If you want to show that your version of Marxism is a cut above somebody else's, the quickest way to do so is to call the other *vulgar*. One's own is sophisticated, subtle, erudite, philosophically rich—all the things the vulgar is not. Or so it has been for a century. Even outside the small world of self-described Marxists, some versions of Marxism have been acceptable in polite company—but rarely the vulgar ones. What is wrong about the vulgar other is a bit of a moving target, as we shall see. The category works by contrast, as the bad term in a combinatory. The sins of the vulgarians are what you claim your refinement of Marxism is a cut above.

When Marx said something was vulgar, he often meant it was bourgeois. This sense of the vulgar is that which has been stripped of its qualities by exchange. But vulgar is a promiscuous word, and sometimes even among Marxists it refers not to the exchangeable thing, but the laboring peoples and the "dirt" that sticks to them one way or another. Does it not seem strange that there are Marxists who want to distance themselves from the vulgar? Does that make them *genteel Marxists*?

Perhaps the very notion that there's something bad about what is vulgar needs challenging. While far from exhausting the multitudinous senses of the word, here are some of the things the vulgar can be: ill-bred, obscene, crude, base, earthy, ordinary, popular, current, vernacular, coarse, common, indelicate, unlettered, idiomatic, heretical. It's curious how this range of meanings also resonates with Blackness or queerness and with that femininity (trans and cis) that finds itself policed rather than idealized.

There are certainly strands of Marxist or Marxist-influenced thought that, while (more or less) respectable, engage with one or other of these senses of the vulgar. At the level of the concept Aimé Cesaire and *negritude*, George Bataille and *base matter*, Raymond Williams and the *ordinary*, Silvia Federici on the *body-politic*—to name just four.[1] At the level of the radical subject, consider Guy Debord and the urban work-shirker, Paul Préciado and the queer sex worker.[2] One could compose a whole countertradition of these affirmative vulgar Marxisms.

In this chapter's thought experiment, let's suppose that getting a conceptual grasp on the twenty-first century might only be possible from the everyday experiences of the various vulgarians who were insulted during the twentieth century. But first, I want to look a bit more closely now at how the insult "vulgar Marxist!" is deployed, and in otherwise not wholly compatible ways, before moving on to four other forms of vulgarity that I think are worth particular attention in the current situation.

Finding the vulgar distasteful is perhaps the defining gesture of so-called *Western Marxism*.[3] For Georg Lukács, the vulgarians think the foundations of bourgeois society are pretty unshakeable. They are in it for the long haul, building unions, mass cultural institutions, and electoral bases.[4] This gradualism in practice corresponds to a theoretical failing. The vulgarian does not take the totality as the central category and sees it as unscientific. Vulgar Marxists reject the doctrine of *commodity fetishism* as the root of a false consciousness that occludes the thought of the totality. They merely practice marxisant flavors of each of the specialized forms of knowledge. A proper dialectical theory grasps History as a totality both as concept and as sphere of action for the proletariat, with the party as the total unifier of theory and practice—or the philosopher.

Karl Korsch thinks the vulgarians do not understand the central importance of the correct dialectical method. They lack a philosophical perspective. For Korsch, as for Lukács, the "orthodox" Marxism of the Second International is the main target of attack. They both dissent from its social theory, where base "mechanically" determines superstructure, and also from its historical theory, which insists on the succession of economic stages and their corresponding political forms. It is too "materialist" a Marxism, not dialectical enough.

Although he had some quirky vulgarian tendencies of his own, Walter Benjamin deploys a slightly different version of the vulgarian insult in "On the Concept of History," worth quoting a little: "The conformism which has dwelt within social democracy from the very beginning rests not merely on its political tactics, but also on its economic conceptions. It is a fundamental cause of the later collapse. There is nothing which has corrupted the German working-class so much as the opinion that *they* were swimming with the tide. Technical developments counted to them as the course of the stream, which they thought they were swimming in. From this, it was only a step to the illusion that the factory-labor set forth by the path of technological progress represented a political achievement. The old Protestant work ethic celebrated its resurrection among German workers in secularized form. The *Gotha Program* already bore traces of this confusion. It defined labor as 'the source of all wealth and all culture.'… This vulgar-Marxist concept of what labor is … wishes to perceive only the progression of the exploitation of nature, not the regression of society… Labor, as it is henceforth conceived, is tantamount to the exploitation of nature, which is contrasted to the exploitation of the proletariat with naïve self-satisfaction."[5]

Benjamin is resistant to the working class point of view of proletarian culture. From Joseph Dietzgen comes what one might call the myth of labor as a key resource for self-organization.[6] From the labor point of view, how could labor come into its own if it did not imagine itself as the source of value? In Korsch and Lukács, what is vulgar lacks a proper understanding of philosophy. Here in Benjamin, interestingly, is a distancing from a positive sense of the vulgar, as the self-image of the working class. And not entirely without justice, but if we are indeed to be dialecticians, perhaps now is the time to negate the negation and return a rude prole stare to this genteel gaze.

Adorno deploys the vulgar insult in a different way. In *Minima Moralia* he claims that the critique of ideology as false consciousness has itself become an ideology.[7] The vulgar Marxist reduction of the cultural artifact to its basic economic determinants comes too close to paralleling the culture industry's own evaluation of its products by their sales numbers. That which in culture might escape exchange value also escapes the vulgar Marxist's attention. For Adorno, as for Lukács and Korsch, what is vulgar lacks a proper understanding of Hegelian dialectics, but for Adorno the dialectic needs an extra twist: absent the revolution, eternal Capital remains a false totality.

Maurice Merleau-Ponty concurs with Lukács's Hegelian-Marxist variant of the insult: The vulgarians neglect the central concept of *totality*.[8] By the time we get to Althusser, it is precisely the dialectic that is vulgar! For Althusser, those vulgarians think of the economic base as an essence and the superstructures as mere appearances. Moreover, they miss Marx's crucial intervention in his critique of the economics of David Ricardo. Marx did not simply take over the object of economic science and bring a "dialectical" method to it. He constructs a whole new and properly "scientific" theoretical object.

While Althusser sees dialectics as the taint of the vulgar, this is still in the name of a genteel Marxism that calls for more, not less, engagement in philosophy. If for Lukács the genteel Marxist has to bring dialectics to Marxism, for Althusser the genteel Marxist has to undo the vulgarizing effects of that dialectics in the name of a better sense of the correct method, but which is still a philosophical method.[9]

E. P. Thompson is famous for a book-length tirade against Althusser.[10] Yet even in Thompson there is a tactical deployment of the vulgarian insult. In his appreciation of Christopher Caudwell, what Thompson finds vulgar is a lack of respect for disciplinary boundaries and hierarchies.[11] This is not that different from Althusser's anxiety about Marxists working in newfangled forms of knowledge such as the study of communication, who he insists need to have the objects of their field defined and policed by Marxist philosophy. In both Thompson and Althusser, there's a sovereign form of knowledge: For Thompson, history is the queen of the sciences; for Althusser, philosophy is king.

This sense of the vulgar other as having tracked their muddy footprints across the disciplines and not followed the protocols of its sovereign form is different to its sense in Lukács or Merleau-Ponty where to be vulgar is to lack a sense of the whole, although both of the latter will claim in turn to have the more elevated means of affecting the synthesis. They are all variants of the genteel gesture of reserving to itself a sovereign role for a more refined Marxism, with access to a special method or perspective.

There are then four general actions of othering involved in calling a Marxism *vulgar*. The first is political. The vulgarians think in terms of a gradual or evolutionary process of historical change. They lack a taste for the political leap. The second is theoretical. The vulgarians pay too much attention to specialized knowledge such as the sciences. They lack the sovereign method. The third is cultural. The vulgarians are too close to the culture of the subordinate classes. They lack a sophistication about the struggle within bourgeois culture. The fourth is more strictly academic. The vulgarian ranges too promiscuously across disciplinary knowledge and lacks training in a traditional knowledge-form that is sovereign.

All of these uses of the vulgarian insult are designed to produce a certain autonomy and priority for the genteel Marxist in relation to the working class. Marxism can't be vulgar, because then the subordinate classes might figure out how to apply it for themselves to their own situation. Marxism also has to be something superior to the sciences, otherwise actual scientists, engineers, designers, media producers, or technical people more generally would have to be acknowledged as co-producers of knowledge. Genteel Marxism can't prioritize the nexus between labor, technology, and nature, as that would pretty much exclude text-based, interpretive forms of knowing such as philosophy or history from claiming a sovereign role. On the other hand, Marxism can't claim to critique scholarly knowledge from without. That would concede too much to those trained (as I was) in the party schools, or with organic experience with emerging forces of production.

If you'll pardon a moment of twenty-first century vulgarity: track Anglophone usage of "vulgar+marxism" in Google's *ngram*, and one finds that its use ramps up steadily through the seventies and then declines in the eighties.[12] The seventies was the time when Lukács, Korsch, Benjamin, Althusser, and many other Western Marxists were translated into English and became textbooks for academic study.

After the decline of the last wave of first-world struggles against Fordist forms of industrial production, Marxism took refuge in the superstructures, particularly in the expanding world of higher education and state-subsidized high culture industries.

There is a new range of extensions and developments of the insult in and after this peak period. Antonio Negri thinks the vulgarians limit themselves to an objectivist and economistic Marxism and fail to understand the potential for revolutionary subjectivity. He even has the wit to hint at the vulgarity of Marx's *Capital* itself, which in his view falls away from the integration of objective and subjective aspects of the *Grundrisse*.[13] Kojin Karatani criticizes as vulgar those Marxisms that take Marx's economics to be an extension of Ricardo's, whereas Ernesto Laclau declares that the vulgarians make a philosophical error in thinking the revolutionary moment as one that produces an absolute reconciliation of society with itself, dissolving false appearances. Cornel West sees the vulgarian as the essentialist and reductionist Marxist who thinks of action entirely as force and does not understand the discursive nature of the political.[14]

Fredric Jameson defends himself against "avant-garde art critics" who "quickly identified me as a vulgar Marxist hatchet man." In some of his most popular works, Terry Eagleton frequently distances his own method from vulgar Marxism, which he puts in scare quotes. Writers otherwise as different as Samir Amin and Julia Kristeva share a disdain for vulgarians, who they think adhere to a mechanistic and deterministic basic metaphor for conceiving the social and historical.[15] In an original move, Jean Baudrillard takes up Walter Benjamin's disdain for proletarian culture's celebration of labor as vulgar but pairs it with genteel Marxism's attempt to critique what labor becomes under capitalism. To him, both positions already concede too much to capitalism as an economic order, which creates this fetish of commodity production in the first place.[16]

The vulgarian insult lived on past the high point of genteel Marxism in the seventies. Perhaps part of what happened is that as Marxism became a creature of the academy, it became a habit to cordon off respectable approaches to Marxist knowledge that could fit within disciplines. In the absence of first-world working class movements that could even appear to effect social change, hope retreated to the academy or other cultural superstructures.

But there was another driver as well: Social movements such as feminism and gay liberation refused to settle for secondary status as mere epiphenomenon to the class struggle. However, the locus for articulating the centrality of these movements was sometimes positioned as outside of productive relations. The terrain of language, or the social or domestic and reproductive relations became the new site of both conceptual and practical struggle. Making the case for such a locus sometimes proceeded through a distancing from vulgar Marxism, to which a relentlessly economic and class-centric approach would be imputed.

Times change, however. Coming out of the theory wars of the eighties, Gayle Rubin seems more concerned about "vulgar Lacanians."[17] By the mid-nineties, Laura Mulvey is surveying the media and culture industries and almost longing for a rather vulgar Marxism to return: "This Marx would no doubt have reflected with interest on the Rupert Murdoch phenomena. For most of my intellectual life, such simple correlations would have fallen into the category of vulgar Marxism. Nowadays the gap of determination between economic structures and culture seems to be narrowing."[18]

Particularly in the era of climate change, revisiting vulgar Marxism might be timely. Lukács disqualified the sciences as fetishes of the particular, unable to grasp the totality, over which only the nonscience of philosophy had dominion. John Bellamy Foster has provided a whole missing lineage of those Marxists who were excluded from the genteel canon for one kind of vulgarity or other, including Engels, Bogdanov, Bukharin, and many lesser known lights who took the heavy, sweaty, gritty engagement of labor and technology with nature, and the sciences that make all that possible, as objects of attention.[19]

Genteel Marxism is a wannabe sovereign discourse, usually a traditional one like philosophy, rather than a more collaborative and comradely production of knowledge. The sciences and social sciences are taken to be specialized, instrumental, to reify their object. One finds variants of this genteel strategy in Negri, Karatani, and Žižek. (Žižek's jokes are vulgar; his philosophy is not.[20]) But this is surely an outdated view of the sciences, based on a critique of its nineteenth century form. As I argued in *Molecular Red*, climate science has to be addressed as being, for better or worse, a science of the totality.[21]

As a way of counterprogramming against genteel Marxism, I want to look at some peculiar instances of the vulgar kind: two about the twenties, two from the sixties. Andrey Platonov (who was that rare thing, the great modernist writer with proletarian origins) wrote a masterpiece, *Chevengur*, which can be read as many things.[22] My attention here is to its vulgar Marxist side. It's an allegorical counter-history of the Soviet Union from the October Revolution through the civil war until the New Economic Policy, but seen from the points of view of characters who are not even proletarian. They are orphans. This is not history from below but history from below the below.

Chevengur does not present the October Revolution from the point of view of the edicts issued from the center, but from their noisy, incoherent reception in the provinces. Platonov's characters perform their own *détournement* of Soviet Marx-speak. Far from revolution as the figurative locomotive of history, actual locomotives collide head-on due to confused signaling. This world is not in transition between modes of production as there is hardly any production at all.

There is hardly a working class in Platonov, but there are comrades. The comrades are those who face the same dangers, the same exposure to the relentless, disorganizing inertia of exposure to the world.[23] Humans and machines, plants and animals can all be comrades. All wear away into nothingness in time. The revolution is supposed to harness all these energies, organize them, inform them, and in the process render them productive. But the tension in Platonov is that hardship and poverty first make comrades. Safety and surplus feed the soul and stimulate private demands. The problem is to restore comradeship beyond the minimal threshold of survival and scarcity.

There can be no end of history in Platonov's world, because nature never lets up, is never conquered, is never providence. Time wears everything away. Communism is always and only a horizon, a minimal line between a blank sky and an empty land. Platonov's characters live on through *secondary ideas*, which can be made actual in the here and now.[24] They work on food security or on irrigation, as Platonov did himself during the famine years of the civil war. Platonov sticks close to the point of view of those whose work it is to hoe the fields, to run the railways, those who find their own ways to be comrades. Platonov's vulgar Marxism is neither total revolutionary leap nor social democratic gradualism. It's a practice of everyday life.

The movement between genteel and vulgar Marxism plays out strongly in the work of Angela Davis. She studied philosophy with Herbert Marcuse in the sixties but was also a militant in the Black Liberation Movement. Davis: "If I still retained any of the elitism which almost inevitably insinuates itself into the minds of college students, I lost it all in the course of the [Black Panther Party] political education sessions."[25] I want to focus on her study of Black women blues singers of the twenties.[26] What she hears in the recordings of Ma Rainey and Bessie Smith is a Black working class sensibility, appearing through fissures within patriarchal language. Black working class culture had little access to writing and publishing, but through its blues singers it did find a way to leave a recorded trace of its oral language, even if at the time few heard it outside of Black proletarian culture. Davis: "As music entered its age of mechanical reproduction, blues were deemed reproducible only within the cultural borders of their site of origin."[27]

Slave society had controlled sexual relations between Black people. The abolition of slavery revolutionized Black personal relationships. Questions of Black sexuality could not be addressed through musical forms of the slavery era. Its spirituals invoked a possible world of collective redemption, at once otherworldly and temporal. It was sacred universe, all-embracing, an imagined community of hope. It was less religion as the opium of the people, and more the heart of a heartless world, to give two of Marx's alternate formulations (the first a *détournement* from Heine).[28]

Out of the frustrated hopes of emancipation came a more exclusively upward-looking redemption in the form of gospel music and a lowly, earthy one, in the blues. God and the Devil found their separate forms, with the Devil having dominion over matters of love and sex. It was not the secular nature of the blues that drew church ire, but their sacred quality. Blues women created a space to preach about sexuality outside of male-dominated church culture.

In the blues, love is not idealized. Freely chosen sexual love is a mediation between emancipation from slavery and new forms of class oppression. Very little in the blues is about marriage and domesticity. Blues women were disinterested in the cult of motherhood and deal frankly with abuse and abandonment. They announce female desire, and it crosses the public–private distinction. They affirm an emotional community and Black humanity. They are frank about lesbian and gay existence.

The blues are not a politics, but for Davis they are a cultural preparation for the political movement to which her own lifelong activism belongs. They anticipate the feminist principle that the personal is political. They counsel financial independence for women and prefer men who work to parasitic ones. And if all else fails, move on. They touch on natural disasters, such as floods, and what that experience means for oppressed and invisible communities. The blues are also frank about sex work and the risks of prosecution and prison. They are the music of those among the subordinate classes who experience the repressive state apparatus as often as the ideological one.

Davis: "Women's blues contested black bourgeois notions of 'high' culture that belittled working class popular music."[29] Upwardly mobile and urban Black culture distanced itself from blues culture. Billie Holiday, the study of whom concludes Davis's book, brought the blues sensibility into her interpretations of the white popular song that displaced the blues. Holiday's work is a *détournement* of white culture industry material to her purposes. Davis does the same for critical theory. She appropriates from her teacher Herbert Marcuse the concept of the *aesthetic dimension* but makes it more vulgar.[30] Here it is the low art of the blues where aesthetics creates the form in which the overcoming of everyday experience can become palpable. The world made over in the form of art can be recognized as an aspect of reality distorted by reality.

Blues songs are collective property, the commons.[31] Davis makes the aesthetic dimension collective and vulgar and connects it to the African practice of the naming of things as a kind of power. Art (and one might add theory) does not achieve greatness by transcending its milieu, but rather is at its best when it opens a dimension within it, brings people to solidarity with each other and the world, while refusing the happy ending—as Holiday does with "Strange Fruit."

For Angela Davis, her sustained encounter with the vulgar took the form of her long involvement with the politics of prison abolition, particularly for and with working class Black women within the prison industrial complex.[32] For Pier Paolo Pasolini, it was more a matter of sexual taste that led him to spend his nights with the *ragga*ʒ*i di vita*, the lively lads, of subproletarian Rome.[33] If for Adorno it was high culture that could preserve a moment before capitalist commodification, for Pasolini it was low—not the remnants of a genteel world, but a peasant one.

Pasolini—poet, novelist, and journalist—was a militant worker in the written language. One of his many interests was the vulgar tongue. Then he moved into cinema and rethought his whole practice. It's his writings on cinema that are my focus here.[34] These took as their starting point the linguistic and semiotic theory popular at the time and made their own vulgar sense out of it.

He started by making a distinction between what he calls *spoken-written* language and *spoken-only* language. Spoken-written Italian is an artifact of the superstructures, of education, literature, administration. Spoken-only language in the Italy of the sixties still included its numerous dialects. These remain from premodern forms of social production. Spoken-only language is the language of the base. Its American equivalents might include the spoken-only Black English that emerged out of slavery and that for Davis is incorporated into the recorded sound of the blues. Spoken-only language mediates between labor and nature.

The rise of what Pasolini calls *neo-capitalism* changes this. From it comes a series of new technical languages of the base. They don't come from the ideological apparatuses of school, church, literature, and so forth. It's the factories that become the unifiers of language. Their form of communication is not necessarily rational, but it is more abstract and more efficient. These new languages of the base replace spoken-only languages with ones derived not from the ideological superstructures but from audio-visual technology. They emerge out of the forces of production.

What drives neo-capitalism, and hence its modifications of language, is an *internal revolution*. The external revolution, the negation of capitalism by the subordinate classes, did not come to pass. Pasolini grasps a key point here: that the working class failed to transform capitalism does not mean that nobody else did. Among the effects of this internal revolution is a transformation of languages from the base up, which succeeded. The attempt by the external revolution to occupy the ideological apparatuses and build a counterhegemonic culture from the superstructures down had already been superseded. Genteel Marxism is marooned in outmoded superstructures.

The new hegemonic language was actually that of what Pasolini calls a *neo-bourgeoisie*, owners of the forces of production out of which these languages emerge. Technical languages replace obsolete spoken-only ones as the language of production. They also displace the literary and administrative languages of the national-cultural superstructure. A new kind of vulgar tongue displaces both an old one and an obsolete form of genteel language.

Pasolini changed his tactics to meet this situation. His essays on language are written in the new technical language of semiotics—how advertising copy writers will henceforth be trained—rather than in the old rhetorical forms. But his main response is cinema. He sees cinema as a technical language that is not dependent on the national-cultural preoccupations of the superstructure. Cinema is the common dream of technocrat and technical worker (although he was perhaps not attentive to the internal contradiction between those two kinds of emerging class subject).[35]

His intervention in cinema is to make, from the base up and using technical language, a replacement for spoken-only language. He made mythic films, in and against neo-capitalism, using its own techniques. One thing that is distinctive about neo-capitalism is that it mass produces subjects in much the same way as it mass produces objects.[36] It makes consumers to go with its products, and in doing so will more and more bypass the old superstructures in the role of subject formation. Pasolini's project is to work in and against the new modes of the production of such subjects.

To the genteel Marxist everything becomes textual; to Pasolini everything becomes cinematic. Reality has its own language, and it is that of cinema. Human perception is like a short cut from the language of the real itself. Cinema is the written language and reality is a "spoken" language. Both human perception and individual films are orderings, cut from the real. Collective human action is a cinema already, of the real, and an individual life is a film.

In neo-capitalism, mechanical reproduction becomes the common form of "spoken" everyday life. Action until now had been spoken only, cinema makes it written. Reality is a cinema of nature. Everyday life is a continuous sequence shot that ends with a cut, with death. Cinema is a way to write these shots, edit them, and combine their points of view. The possibility of an objective "take" on the real is between the shots. The objective extends beyond the subjective point of view, in art as well as science.

Editing does for film what death does for life. Both introduce the possibility of meaning. Cinema, which wants to be false, can't help being real. But the real is a nonhuman mystery, and is inescapable. All communication is sacred, giving meaning to the real. Cinema cuts into the continuous time of the real, giving it meaning. Films, like lives, are mortal. But cinema is immortal and sacred. Cinema is bound to life. Pasolini was queer for time, for the raw, vulgar, sacred time of the world. Only the genteel make a fetish of language and make language itself sacred. This is Pasolini's vulgar Marxist *heretical empiricism*, his distance from both genteel Marxism and from the (for him equally genteel) avant-garde.[37]

As with the genteel Marxisms, Pasolini extracts his worldview from his own labor process. At least in his case, working in cinema and mass media gave him insight into an emerging moment in the development of capitalism, one where perhaps it was starting to become something else, driven by an internal revolution among its ruling classes, the external challenge to its power by labor having failed. He struggled in and against the audiovisual forces of cultural production of his time and tried to open a vulgar, common, aesthetic dimension within it that looked back to premodern, precommodified forms of everyday life. But this recourse to the archaic did not make him a subtle reader of emerging class antagonisms and alliances, and for that I want to turn to our fourth vulgarian, his contemporary Asger Jorn.

Jorn's Marxism is not that of either the working class or the genteel writer. He was an artist. His was a socialism that is neither utopian nor scientific, but experimental. Jorn thought the sources of aesthetic creation were popular and was in his own way quite content to call himself a vulgar Marxist.[38] He developed a novel vulgar Marxism as a critique of some of the more prevalent kinds of vulgar Marxism that I examined earlier. He thought that (vulgar) Marxists left something out of the equation of labor with value. Jorn restored a role for nature, for materiality, and also for producers of form, for what he jokingly called a *creative elite*. The term is ironic. Artists are the opposite of a power elite.[39] In a commodity economy, they have no power. Art is supposed to give form to the social practices of life, but in a commodity economy, art is cut off from life and becomes a special kind of commodity instead.

Where Pasolini was disturbed by the expansion of wealth under neo-capitalism, Jorn saw no expansion of wealth at all. What has value in Jorn is difference, whereas commodity production just makes more and more sameness. Capital has impoverished the world. Far from being a critique, Marx's scientific socialism reduces the complexity and difference of form to a rational essence. Marx lacks a sense of the materiality of forms (or one might add, information: the form of materiality is information).

Marxism is all too often reduced to a dialectic of form and essence. The essence of value is labor. But for Jorn, form is not a container for a content or essence. Bourgeois thought sees only exchange, and Marx lifts the veil and shows how value is produced before it is exchanged. Jorn lifts another veil, revealing not those who fill the form with content, but those who change those forms and produce difference itself.

Capital alienated labor from creation, separating the production of content from the differentiation of forms. Actually existing socialist economies did not solve the problem, with their obsession with increasing quantities of production alone. Rather than the party (or its philosophers) bringing class consciousness from without, Jorn wants a horizontal relation between artist and worker.

Jorn drew a distinction between the *materialist worldview* and the *materialist attitude to life*.[40] He thought Marx had the former but not the latter. A Marxism in rude health needs both. A materialist attitude to life would be open-ended and experimental, but also collective and practical. While he generally through artists had been cut off from the role of form giver, the blues as Davis presents it might be the kind of materialist attitude to life that is also form giving. But where for Davis, such a form negates everyday experience and opens the possibility of a politics, for Jorn form can also affirm everyday experience and give a new shape to it. His conception of historical change has a directly aesthetic dimension.

Drawing together all four of our instances of the vulgar, what I suggest is this: first, an orientation toward the intractable difficulties of organizing the world through labor (Platonov); second, a feeling for the sources of social change directly in the mediated experience of the most marginalized and oppressed (Davis); third, a practice of working in and against the technical forms of the time (Pasolini); and fourth, thinking one's own everyday creative experience, when it involves the production of novel forms, as not that of labor, but as that of another kind of subordinate class (Jorn).

This (affirmative, experimental, collaborative) vulgar Marxist approach then reveals genteel Marxism as formed by its own habits of work. Genteel Marxism was mostly a product of forms of textual study, in traditional fields such as philosophy, history, and literature. It projects the norms of that labor as metaphors onto the world. Written language is not a good medium in which to grasp the intractability of the world, the practico-inert. Nor is it good on the subtle affective dimension of everyday culture and is in particular not a good place from which to understand how traditional textual forms were superseded by the development of media technics itself.

Genteel Marxism withdrew into the superstructures. It found itself overvaluing traditional forms, in a pastoral husbanding of bourgeois styles. It found itself favoring notions of the political or the cultural that the internal revolution of commodity production had rendered residual. And not least, genteel Marxism locks onto the received idea that this is in essence still capitalism, with capitalism's temporary relations of class domination erected into an absolute.

Two things remain rather hastily elided, even if they are sore points that keep coming up. One is the relation of genteel Marxists, trained in the writerly techniques (be they of literature, philosophy, or law), with others trained in practices of creating and verifying information that are not writerly. How is the writerly connected (or not) to the technical fields or to competence in media other than the written and spoken word? In what way is writing as a competence a mark of a certain kind of gentility itself? The Man of Letters leaves it to somebody else to type them and post them.[41] His inheritors can't even put up their own blog posts in WordPress.

The other elided problem is the writerly intellectual's relation to the working class. Being in the party of the working class or a fellow traveler of it appears to solve this problem, for genteel Marxists as different as Lukács, Sartre, and Althusser. Another solution, derived from Lukács, is to be the custodian of the totality. The genteel Marxist becomes the spokesman for History itself. One can also find this solution in Jameson, Karatani, or Žižek, and in a particularly elegant form in Paolo Virno.[42]

A frequent gesture is to make the connection between the genteel authority of the writerly, particularly as that authority is shaped by the university or by a high literary culture, and the authentic mission of labor at the expense of other kinds of information production practice. The philosophical or the literary is then the guarantee of some critical acumen that the genteel bestows upon labor as a kind of noblesse oblige. But the key thing for our purposes is that this has a double effect. The first is this cathecting onto the destiny of labor of something foreign to it, a genteel learnedness. The second is the reciprocal use of this imaginary connection to labor to claim to possess something that other kinds of intellectual labor lack.

The genteel Marxist claims to know and negate bourgeois culture and then to represent it metaphorically to the working class. By identifying metaphorically with labor as a whole, Marxist intellectuals evade the question of their own class location and the extent to which it may be shared with others whose immediate labor processes are otherwise quite different. The metaphoric inversion impedes the possibility of thinking metonymically, that they are just a part of some other subaltern class. Thus, it is often hard to forge links between the literary or philosophical Marxist intellectual and progressive movements in fields that are technical or scientific—that other and (in many ways more important) fraction of the hacker class.

This may be particularly detrimental at a time when all fractions of the hacker class face similar problems. Our work is made routine, is deskilled, becomes precarious and casualized. It is absorbed into the same logics of vectoral power. We can't practice solidarity among our own class. We are deduced to belonging to little (Durkheimian) groups, hoarding our (Weberian) opportunities. This is particularly worrying at a time when *both* the humanities and the sciences are under attack by new kinds of irrationalism fostered and funded by regressive sections of the ruling class such as the fossil fuel industry. At the same time, they (we) find our creative and productive activities more and more subordinated to forms of information management and control, which may indeed be more abstract ways of organizing hacker activity but are by no means more rational.

It has also made it difficult to keep abreast of developments in the forces of production. It takes actual technical knowledge or situated experience to understand how these things work. That knowledge tends to be specialized. It takes a whole practice of collaborative intellectual labor to pool such knowledge and understand the shape of the forces of production as they emerge, in terms other than those favored by the ruling class. This is a major front in the politics of knowledge of today.

And so: four cheers for vulgar Marxism!!!! Four rather than three, as the vulgar is always a little excessive.[43] Four cheers for these four vulgar Marxist writers, although they are also much more than that. Opening up the vulgar wing of the archive again might open some more plural pathways through which to think from past to present, to inhabitable futures.

Marxism needs to be vulgar again, but perhaps in a different way. The leading edge of development of the forces of production is not the industrial system any more.[44] They develop now across a wide range of science and engineering fields. The development of new forces of production has for some time now not been left to chance, but is itself organized in a whole parallel regime of commodification. Put simply, the worker is subsumed into the manufacture of sameness; the hacker is subsumed into the production of difference. It turns out that genteel Marxists belonged to a minor branch of the latter, as a subculture.

Conclusion: A Night at the Movies

> Oh, my dear, dear darling,
> now you even start meddling in politics.
> That is the most daredevil undertaking.
>
> —Jenny von Westphalen

Many of my friends disliked it, and not without reason. And yet Raoul Peck's film *The Young Karl Marx* seemed to me to get the essential thing right.[1] I saw it as a film about the struggle to live in the present. As such, it's a film that can help us do exactly that. *The Young Karl Marx* is fiction, but like all good fiction is more real than the documentary evidence on which it is based. It tells us not what actually happened, but a version of what happened with which to think what is happening now. In that sense, it is a species of realism.[2] And in another sense too. It is a work of cinema. It is in Pasolini's terms (and Barad's also) cut from the real itself.

There are four characters: There is the young couple, Karl and Jenny Marx. There is Karl's new best friend, Friedrich Engels, and Freddy's new special friend, Mary Burns. Each needs the other to find their way into the present and out of the past. They are comrades in the struggle to be of their time. Jenny needs Karl to escape her genteel family, but Karl needs Jenny to guide him toward what is urgent. Fred needs Karl to most clearly write what it is they are coming to perceive in the world. Karl needs Fred because of his money. But not just that. He needs what Fred has found out about a world that is coming into existence.

Fred, the son of a mill owner, has seen the new forces of production. Fred needs Mary to discover what a textile mill owner's son cannot see. He needs her to discover the city, to wander outside of his class. Does Mary need Fred? Well, the vulgar answer would be yes, because he is loaded. The more allegorical answer would be that the working class needs a concept of its form and its possibilities, and that may have to come from without.

The four comrades find their way to the present through a struggle with those who are struggling in the ways of the past. In Germany, the progressive bourgeois are still trying to make their revolution against the old landlord class, even as the landlord class is still in the process of putting its relation to the peasantry on a more abstract and strictly cash basis. Karl has to part ways with those who are still caught up in the task of the critique of the old ruling class and its ideology—religion.

In Paris, Karl and Jenny find what seems like a more congenial radicalism, about politics rather than religion. But it too is not quite of the present. Proudhon's theories and Weitling's grand speeches address the artisan rather than the factory worker. They are rooted in eternal and more or less Christian appeals to justice. They are not of their time. Fred's book *The Condition of the Working Class in England* touches on the world as it is coming into being, and that has to be the place to begin to imagine once again what the Grand Old Cause of the people might become.[3] Fred gets Karl to read the English political economists. Neither German culture nor French politics is quite of the present: English economics just might be.

Fred and Karl are still genteel critics of their world, writing satirical hot takes on their elders and peers. In the movie, the link back to the world and to the present comes through Mary, the Irish mill-worker, who ushers them in to the League of the Just. These rough-handed men, who have taken their share of beatings, live by the creed All Men Are Brothers. Theirs is a vulgar and deeply felt commitment to equality. But they don't have a program. They lack contacts. They think beyond the national but don't have the means to make that commitment concrete.

The film's climactic scene is one that could be loved only by those of us who have sat and stood, shouted and cursed, laughed and sang and drank our way through our share of political meetings in dusty halls, in the backs of pubs, in somebody's kitchen. After the inevitable quibble about accreditation, Fred takes the podium and announces a new program. The League of the Just will henceforth be known as the Communist League. It is put to a vote and carries the day. Mary replaces the old rainbow banner over the window with the fresh red one as weak sun streams in behind it.

If one has lived through even a small and petty version of such events, then one knows what comes next. Having won the vote, our faction now has to write the document that embodies the will of the meeting that it is to express. Karl is procrastinating, as he does. Fred tries to convince him to put aside his day job as a precarious correspondent for foreign newspapers. The film comes almost to a close with a fantastic scene in which Fred, Karl, Jenny, and Mary get drunk and scribble lines for the *Communist Manifesto* by candlelight. The revolutions of 1848 are just a month away. Workers of the world unite! You have a world to win!

Peck ends his film with a montage and a Bob Dylan song. Having pushed our four comrades into the present (1848), the montage smash-cuts History to the end of the twentieth century and the becoming of this rather less appealing sequel century. The question it leaves me with is: can we be in this present as Karl and Jenny and Fred and Mary were in theirs? This time is not their time. Here the realism of the film pulls against its naturalism. The clothes, the streets, the furniture, Fred's office and the family factory, the bar where Mary drinks with the Irish, the post office where Karl is refused a job on account of his terrible handwriting—it all feels dated and a little bit too neatly crafted. The mise-en-scène is somehow not quite right.

The naturalistic details are about a past even to our hero-comrades' past. It is the practico-inert against which they fling themselves. Everything they say and do tries to call into being a present that all that jumble and tat pulls back into stasis and inertia. Karl is trying to write about the real yet abstract forces that warp and weft these appearances into being. Karl is trying to write about it as a present that could be open to other futures, ones not prophesized in the eternal verities of the League of the Just.

Peck gives us a naturalistic world within the frame of the 1840s, a world that appears as an accumulation of commodities and of the labor that makes them. Into that setting, he insinuates the birth of a realism of the concept that articulated what made it and what could be made of what made it. Then he gives us, right at the very end, the naturalistic world of the 2010s, a world that appears as an accumulation of images and of the everyday life that appears within those images. We know, having seen how our four comrades come to know this, that the naturalistic surfaces are produced by abstract forces. But the naturalistic surfaces are different. *So too must be the abstract forces.* This is no longer the world of Karl and Jenny, Fred and Mary.

Behind the surfaces lies not eternal Capital, but something else. The whole point of our four comrades' struggle has been to step out of finding solace once again in unseen essences. Their struggle was to live in the present. To me, that is the challenge of the film: that we have to live in our own time. This is why it is a film about young people, addressed to young people. The present of our present still needs to be written.

I took my kids to see it. I wanted them to know something of the origins and motivations of a structure of feeling that was something that I once felt deeply and to which I will remain in solidarity for the rest of my life. Let us admit, comrades, that we are a defeated people. There will be no second coming for us. And to try to remain in fidelity to something whose core myth lies in History is always to betray it anyway. The whole is to be begun again, and from the beginning.

To be an atheist is to reject the existence of God, and yet the possibility of such nonbelief is defined negatively, by the thing it knows not to be actual or possible. To be an *acommunist*, likewise. The a-suffix simply means without, not against. The old banner will have to come down someday, and the old manifesto put back in the archive, left to the gnawing criticism of the scholars.

What is still to be achieved is the struggle to grasp the surface effects of the present through concepts that articulate the abstract forces that produce them, forces that are not eternal and are not an essence. It can't be done by means of words alone. Words have to connect to everyday life in all its vulgar glory and idiocy, and right at the point where the emerging forces of production are shaping that everyday life, riven perhaps by quite distinctive forms of class struggle and experience. The means to live and endure otherwise may already have come into existence, fettered though they are by outmoded relations and forms.

Workings of the world untie! You have a win to world!

Acknowledgments

The working method for this book was to start with some published articles; laminate them together; and then cut, hammer, and oxy-weld them into the shape of a book. The chapters are much changed from their original forms.

Some of the text I have repurposed from occasional pieces for *Public Seminar*. Also in the mix is part of an essay for the *Museum of Capitalism* book, published by Inventory Press (2017). Other bits appeared thanks to eflux in their *Supercommunity* project for the 56th Venice Biennale (2015) and in the print journal *Counter-Signals*, no. 3 (2018). Another part appeared in *Multitudes*, no. 70 (2018). I also used text that was commissioned for *The Bloomsbury Companion to Marx* (2018) by Jeff Diamanti, Andrew Pendakis, and Imre Szeman, as well as some text that was commissioned for the book *Former West: Art and the Contemporary After 1989*, edited by Maria Hlavajova et al. and published by MIT Press in 2017. Another chunk was commissioned by the Chinese language journal *Leap*. I may also have used material from a commission by Raqs Media Collective to write a "theory opera" for the 11th Shanghai Biennale (2016).

Some of this material was presented at the *Marx Now Symposium* at the Goethe Institut in New York, May 5, 2018. My thanks to the New

Political Science section for allowing me to present some of this work as their plenary lecture at the American Political Science Association, which was published in its journal *New Political Science* in 2017. My thanks to the fellows of the Heilbroner Center for Capitalism Studies at The New School for workshopping it with me.

The manuscript benefitted from editorial suggestions by John Merrick and from my Verso point-person Leo Hollis. Remaining shortcomings will be due to my failure to take their advice.

Special thanks to the students at New School for Social Research, none of whom necessarily agree with any of the theses of this book but from all of whom I have learned a lot: Sam Tobin, Phillip Kalantzis-Cope, Zeyno Ustun, Liliana Gil, and Andy Moon, and in particular my recent students in Liberal Studies: Macushla Robinson, Ben Kodres-O'Brien, Elvia Wilk, Michael Smaczylo, Michael Sonni Mason, Leo Zausen, Tom Ward, Chris Ianos, and Amanda Parmer. Extra special thanks to Krista Trieu, my research assistant.

Notes

Introduction

1 Bernard Harcourt, *Exposed: Desire and Disobedience in the Digital Age*, Cambridge, MA: Harvard University Press, 2015.

2 Dallas Smythe, "Communications: Blind Spot of Western Marxism," *Canadian Journal of Political and Social Theory* 1: 3, 1977, 1–28; Sut Jhally, *The Codes of Advertising*, New York: Routledge, 1990.

3 Yves Citton, *The Ecology of Attention*, Cambridge, UK: Polity Press, 2017.

4 David Ogilvy, *Confessions of an Advertising Man*, London: Southbank, 2012.

5 There are strategies for minimizing that information's utility: Finn Brunton and Helen Nissenbaum, eds., *Obfuscation: A User's Guide for Privacy and Protest*, Cambridge, MA: MIT Press, 2015.

6 Siva Vaidhayanathan, *Antisocial Media*, New York: Oxford University Press, 2018; Siva Vaidhayanathan, *The Googlization of Everything*, Berkeley: University of California Press, 2012.

7 Theodor Adorno, *The Culture Industry: Selected Essays on Mass Culture*, New York: Routledge, 2001.

8 Jonathan Crary, *24/7: Later Capitalism and the Ends of Sleep*, New York: Verso, 2014.

9 Xavier Cannone, *Surrealism in Belgium: 1924–2004*, London: Thames & Hudson, 2007.

10 David Graeber, *Debt: The First 5,000 Years*, New York: Melville House, 2014.

11 Seb Franklin, *Control: Digitality as Cultural Logic*, Cambridge, MA: MIT Press, 2015.

12 I have adapted the concept of vector from Paul Virilio, *Aesthetics of Disappearance*, Los Angeles: Semiotext(e), 2009.

13 Cathy O'Neil, *Weapons of Math Destruction*, London: Penguin Books, 2017; Virginia Eubanks, *Automating Inequality*, New York: St. Martins Press, 2018; Frank Pasquale, *The Black Box Society*, Cambridge, MA: Harvard University Press, 2016.

14 Safiya Umoja Noble, *Algorithms of Oppression*, New York: New York University Press, 2018.

15 Jackie Wang, *Carceral Capitalism*, Los Angeles: Semiotext(e), 2018.

16 Paul Dourish, *The Stuff of Bits: An Essay on the Materialities of Information*, Cambridge, MA: MIT Press, 2017.

17 André Gorz, *The Immaterial*, Kolkata: Seagull Books, 2010, offered some forward thinking insights but to my mind got stuck on this image of the emerging forces of production.

18 For a primer on the historical genesis of information, see James Gleick, *The Information*, New York: Vintage, 2012.

19 Some even argue that the universe itself is a computer simulation: Nick Bostrom, "Are We Living in a Computer Simulation?" *Philosophical Quarterly* 53: 211, 2003, 243–55.

20 I see this book as in friendly dialog with Tiziana Terranova, *Network Culture: Politics for the Information Age*, London: Pluto Press, 2004; Matteo Pasquinelli, *Animal Spirits: A Bestiary of the Commons*, Amsterdam: Institute for Network Cultures, 2009; Christian Fuchs, *Digital Labour and Karl Marx*, London: Routledge, 2014; Nick Dyer-Witheford, *Cyber-Proletariat*, London: Pluto Press, 2015; Nick Srnicek and Alex Williams, *Inventing the Future*, London: Verso, 2016; Jonathan Beller, *The Message is Murder: Substrates of Computational Capital*, London: Pluto Press, 2017.

21 Shoshana Zuboff, *The Age of Surveillance Capitalism*, New York: Public Affairs, 2018; Nick Srnicek, *Platform Capitalism*, Cambridge, UK: Polity, 2016; David Kotz, *The Rise and Fall of Neoliberal Capitalism*, Cambridge, MA: Harvard University Press, 2017; Alain Lipietz, *Towards a New Economic Order: Postfordism, Ecology and Democracy*, Oxford: Oxford University Press, 1992.

22 Paul Mason, *Postcapitalism: A Guide to Our Future*, London: Allen Lane, 2015, xix.

23 Ned Rossiter, *Software Infrastructure, Labor: A Media Theory of Logistical Nightmares*, New York: Routledge, 2016.

24 *Fortune 500*, 2017. See Fredric Jameson, *Valences of the Dialectic*, New York: Verso, 2010, 420ff, in which he proposes Walmart's logistics as a dialectically reversible model of socialism.

25 Jesse LeCavalier, *The Rule of Logistics*, Minneapolis: University of Minnesota Press, 2016.

26 Kate Crawford and Vladan Joler, "Anatomy of the AI System," AI Now Institute, September 7, 2018, at anatomyof.ai. Important to mention here that what appears to be automation often hides a great deal of labor. See Astra Taylor, 'The Automation Charade,' *Logic: A Magazine About Technology*, No. 5, 2018. She calls this *fauxtomation*.

27 Benjamin Bratton, *The Stack: On Software and Sovereignty*, Cambridge, MA: MIT Press, 2016.

28 Alexander Galloway, *The Interface Effect*, Cambridge, UK: Polity, 2011.

29 Wendy Hui Kyong Chun, *Updating to Remain the Same: Habitual New Media*, Cambridge, MA: MIT Press, 2017.

30 Phil Neel, *Hinterland: America's New Landscape of Class and Conflict*, London: Reaktion Books, 2018.

31 Vincent Mosco, *To the Cloud: Big Data in a Turbulent World*, New York: Routledge, 2014.

32 Brett Neilson and Sandro Mezzada, *Border as Method, or, the Multiplication of Labor*, Durham, NC: Duke University Press, 2013.

33 Deborah Cowan, *The Deadly Life of Logistics: Mapping Violence in Global Trade*, Minneapolis: University of Minnesota Press, 2014.

34 Heike Geissler, *Seasonal Associate*, Los Angeles: Semiotext(e), 2018 (an account by an artist forced by necessity to take a seasonal job at Amazon).

35 Ernst Bloch, *Atheism in Christianity*, London: Verso, 2009. Bloch's Marxist argument that the kernel of atheism is to be found in Christianity also contains its dialectical reversal.

36 Rather than the end of the grand narratives, perhaps another way of writing them, contra Jean-François Lyotard, *The Postmodern Condition: A Report on Knowledge*, Minnesota: University of Minneapolis Press, 1984.

37 An alternative mode of organization of critical theory, and other things:

Stefano Harney and Fred Moten, *The Undercommons: Fugitive Planning and Black Study*, London: Minor Compositions, 2013.

38 Tom McDonough, *The Beautiful Language of My Century: Reinventing the Language of Contestation in Postwar France*, Cambridge, MA: MIT Press, 2011.

39 McKenzie Wark, *A Hacker Manifesto*, Cambridge, MA: Harvard University Press, 2004.

40 Karl Marx, *The Revolutions of 1848*, London: Verso, 2010; Karl Marx, *Surveys from Exile*, London: Verso, 2010; Karl Marx, *The First International and After*, London: Verso, 2010.

41 Raymond Williams, *The Long Revolution*, Cardigan, UK: Parthian Books, 2011.

42 Noam Chomsky et al., *The Cold War and the University*, New York: The New Press, 1998.

43 For example, consider the way the commodification of life gives new life to the form of the commodity: Melinda Cooper, *Life as Surplus*, Seattle: University of Washington Press, 2008; Kaushik Sunder Rajan, *Biocapital*, Durham, NC: Duke University Press, 2006.

44 Randy Martin, *An Empire of Indifference*, Durham, NC: Duke University Press, 2007; Ivan Asher, *Portfolio Society*, New York: Zone Books, 2016. My thanks to the Volatility Group at The New School for thoughts on this.

45 David Noble, *The Forces of Production*, New York: Oxford University Press, 1986.

46 Erik Olin Wright, *Understanding Class*, New York: Verso, 2015.

47 Lawrence Lessig, *Free Culture*, New York: Penguin, 2015.

48 Rebecca Lowen, *Creating the Cold War University*, Berkeley: University of California Press, 1997.

49 Wendy Brown, *Undoing the Demos: Neoliberalism's Stealth Revolution*, New York: Zone Books, 2017.

50 Paul N. Edwards, *A Vast Machine: Computer Models, Climate Data and the Politics of Global Warming*, Cambridge, MA: MIT Press, 2010.

51 Benjamin Noys, *Malign Velocities: Accelerationism and Capitalism*, Winchester, UK: Zero Books, 2014.

52 John Bellamy Foster, *Marx's Ecology*, New York: Monthly Review Press, 2000.

53 Chun, *Updating to Remain the Same.*

54 Vilém Flüsser, *Towards a Philosophy of Photography*, London: Reaktion Books, 2000, 12.

55 Perry Anderson, *Considerations on Western Marxism*, London: Verso, 1976.

56 Alexander Bogdanov, *The Philosophy of Living Experience*, Chicago: Haymarket, 2017.

57 In practical terms, this would be my problem with the formula of a fidelity to an event as that which creates a political subjectivity. See Alain Badiou, *Ethics: An Essay on the Understanding of Evil*, London: Verso, 2013.

1. The Sublime Language of My Century

1 Just one example from recent popular literature: Bhu Srinivasan, *Americana: A 400-Year History of American Capitalism*, New York: Penguin, 2017.

2 Yann Moulier Boutang, *Cognitive Capitalism*, Cambridge, UK: Polity, 2012; Jodi Dean, *Democracy and Other Neoliberal Fantasies: Communicative Capitalism and Left Politics*, Durham, NC: Duke University Press, 2009; Wendy Brown, *Undoing the Demos*, New York: Zone Books, 2017. Franco Berardi, *Futurability*, London: Verso, 2017. I wrote about all of these in *General Intellects*, London: Verso, 2017.

3 "Modern" here in the sense given it in Henri Lefebvre, *Introduction to Modernity*, London: Verso, 2012: the critical agent in and against the present.

4 Marshall Berman, *All That Is Solid Melts into Air*, New York: Penguin, 1988.

5 Rob Nixon, *Slow Violence*, Cambridge, MA: Harvard University Press, 2013.

6 Gilles Deleuze, *The Logic of Sense*, New York: Columbia University Press, 1990, 155ff.

7 Roland Barthes, *Image, Music, Text*, New York: Hill & Wang, 1977.

8 Jairus Banaji, *Theory as History: Essays on Modes of Production and Exploitation*, Chicago: Haymarket Books, 2011.

9 Keston Sutherland, *Stupefaction: A Radical Anatomy of Phantoms*, Calcutta: Seagull, 2011; Robert Paul Wolff, *Moneybags Must Be So*

Lucky: On the Literary Structure of Capital, Amherst: University of Massachusetts Press, 1988.

10   Hayden White, *Metahistory*, Baltimore, MD: Johns Hopkins University Press, 2014.

11   Kenneth Goldsmith, *Head Citations*, Los Angeles: The Figures, 2002. Apparently a misheard lyric is known as a *mondegreen*.

12   This is what I remember of the catechism I was taught in party school, probably from D. I. Chesnokov, *Historical Materialism*, Moscow: Progress Publishers, 1969.

13   Benjamin Noys, *Malign Velocities: Accelerationism and Capitalism*, Winchester, UK: Zero Books, 2014; J. D. Bernal, *The World, The Flesh and the Devil*, London: Verso Books, 2017.

14   The Prometheus myth has its uses. See Jared Hickman, *Black Prometheus: Race and Radicalism in the Age of Atlantic Slavery*, New York: Oxford University Press, 2016.

15   A particularly striking version of the apologetics for Capital as destiny has it arrive from the future: Nick Land, *Fanged Noumena*, Falmouth, UK: Urbanomic, 2013.

16   Wendy Brown, *Undoing the Demos: Neoliberalism's Stealth Revolution*, New York: Zone Books, 2017.

17   Timothy Brooks, ed., *The Asiatic Mode of Production in China*, London: Routledge, 1989.

18   Fredric Jameson, *Postmodernism, Or, The Cultural Logic of Late Capitalism*, London: Verso, 1992; Paolo Virno, *A Grammar of the Multitude*, Los Angeles: Semiotext(e), 2004; Franco Berardi, *And: Phenomenology of the End*, Los Angeles: Semiotext(e), 2015; Anthony Lowenstein, *Disaster Capitalism*, London: Verso, 2017; Brett Levinson, *Market and Thought: Meditations on the Political and Biopolitical*, New York: Fordham University Press, 2004; Giorgio Grizioti, *Neurocapitalism*, London: Minor Compositions, 2019.

19   Chiara Bottici, *Imaginal Politics*, New York: Columbia University Press, 2014.

20   Maurizio Lazzarato, *Signs and Machines*, Los Angeles: Semiotext(e), 2014.

21   Leslie Chang, *Factory Girls*, New York: Speigel and Grau, 2009.

22   Francis Fukuyama, *The End of History and the Last Man*, New York: Free Press, 2006.

23 Guy Debord, *The Society of the Spectacle*, New York: Zone Books, 1994.

24 Louis Althusser, *For Marx*, London: Verso Books, 2006. On advances in social reproduction theory, see Tithi Bhattacharya, ed., *Social Reproduction Theory: Remapping Class, Recentering Oppression*, London: Pluto Press, 2017.

25 For example: Ferruccio Rossi-Landi, *Marxism and Ideology*, Oxford: Oxford University Press, 1990. Alternately, if the science of the economic base is Marxism, the science of the ideological superstructure is psychoanalysis.

26 For example, Jacques Rancière, *Dissensus: On Politics and Aesthetics*, London: Bloomsbury, 2015.

27 See Tom McDonough, *The Beautiful Language of My Century*, Cambridge, MA: MIT Press, 2007, which for Debord was the language of revolution. The sublime language is some other tongue.

28 The messianic and allegorical version of history came from certain readings of Walter Benjamin, *Illuminations*, New York: Shocken Books, 1969; Walter Benjamin, *Reflections*, New York: Shocken Books, 1986.

29 On defamiliarization as the roof caving in, see Viktor Shklovsky, *Mayakovsky and His Circle*, London: Pluto Press, 1974.

30 An attachment that may be a shared affect more than an individual emotion. Melissa Gregg and Gregory Seigworth, *The Affect Theory Reader*, Durham, NC: Duke University Press, 2010.

31 Richard Barbrook, *Imaginary Futures: From Thinking Machines to the Global Village*, London: Pluto Press, 2008.

32 Theodor Adorno, *The Culture Industry: Selected Essays on Mass Culture*, New York: Routledge, 2001.

33 Joseph Schumpeter, *Capitalism, Socialism and Democracy*, New York: Harper Perennial, 2008.

34 Richard Barbrook, *The Internet Revolution*, Amsterdam: Institute for Network Cultures, 2015.

35 This literature is itself a growth industry; see Jeremy Rivkin, *The Third Industrial Revolution*, New York: St. Martins Press, 2013; Klaus Schwab, *The Fourth Industrial Revolution*, New York: Crown Business, 2017.

36 McKenzie Wark, *A Hacker Manifesto*, Cambridge, MA: Harvard University Press, 2004; McKenzie Wark, *Gamer Theory*, Cambridge, MA: Harvard University Press, 2007.

37 Enzo Traverso, *Left-Wing Melancholia: Marxism, History and Memory*, New York: Columbia University Press, 2017.

38 Raymond Williams, *Resources of Hope*, London: Verso, 1989.

39 Mark Fisher, *Capitalist Realism*, Winchester, UK: Zero Books, 2009.

40 Engels is the source for this bit of table-talk. See, for example, Engels's letter to C. Schmidt in Berlin, August 5, 1850: www.marxists.org/archive/marx/works/1890/letters/90_08_05.htm

41 The founding text of steampunk is William Gibson and Bruce Sterling, *The Difference Engine*, New York: Ballantine Books, 2011. Originally published in 1990, this retro-science fiction novel sometimes seems to correspond to the world some contemporary Marxists seem to think they inhabit.

42 Marshall Berman, *Adventures in Marxism*, New York: Verso, 2010.

43 Raymond Williams, *The Long Revolution*, Cardigan, Wales: Parthian Books, 2012.

44 See Alexander Galloway's contribution in this book, coauthored with Eugene Thacker and McKenzie Wark: *Excommunication: Three Inquiries in Media and Mediation*, Chicago: Chicago University Press, 2013.

45 The most famous supplemental Marxism is perhaps Herbert Marcuse, *Eros and Civilization*, Boston: Beacon Press, 1974: Marx supplemented with Freud.

46 Göran Therborn, *From Marxism to Post-Marxism?* London: Verso, 2018.

47 Michel Foucault, *The Order of Things*, New York: Vintage, 1994, 261–2.

48 Perry Anderson, *Considerations on Western Marxism*, London: Verso, 1979.

49 Roland Barthes, *Elements of Semiology*, New York: Hill & Wang, 1977.

50 Debord, *The Society of the Spectacle*, 145ff.

51 Ibid., 206–208. These passages, needless to say, include détourned phrases from others, including Lautréamont.

52 Karl Marx and Fredrick Engels, *Collected Works Vol. 35: Capital Vol. 1*, New York: International Publishers, 1996, 45; Debord, *The Society of the Spectacle*, 12.

53 Sutherland, *Stupefaction*, 32.

54 Ibid., 33.

55 Marx, *Collected Works, Vol. 35: Capital, Vol. 1*, 81–95.

56 Sutherland, *Stupefaction*, 43.

57 Ibid., 47.

58 Ibid., 36.

59 William Pietz, "The Problem of the Fetish," *RES: Anthropology and Aesthetics* 9: 1, 1985, 5–17.

60 Galloway, *Excommunication*.

61 Gustave Flaubert, *Bouvard and Pechuet with The Dictionary of Received Ideas*, London: Penguin Classics, 1976.

62 A metaphysics one was taught to question in Michel Foucault, *The Archaeology of Knowledge*, New York: Vintage, 1982. Only this in turn became the foundation of its own doxa.

63 Karl Marx, "Preface," *A Contribution to the Critique of Political Economy*, Moscow: Progress Publishers, 1977, https://www.marxists.org/archive/marx/works/1859/critique-pol-economy/preface.htm

64 Ibid.

2. Capitalism—or Worse?

1 Donna Haraway, "The Promises of Monsters," *The Haraway Reader*, New York: Routledge, 2004.

2 Melissa Gregg, *Counterproductive: Time Management in the Knowledge Economy*, Durham, NC: Duke University Press, 2018.

3 Lana Wachowski and Lilly Wachowski (directors), *The Matrix*, Los Angeles: Warner Brothers, 1999.

4 Joss Whedon (executive producer), *The Dollhouse*, Los Angeles: 20th Century Fox Productions, 2009–2010.

5 Arlie Russell Hochschild, *The Managed Heart*, Berkeley: University of California Press, 2011.

6 Jordan Peele (writer and director), *Get Out*, Los Angeles: Blumhouse Productions, 2017.

7 Ann Leckie, *Ancillary Justice*, London: Orbit, 2015.

8 Agustín de Rojas, *The Year 200*, trans. Nick Caistor and Hebe Powell, New York: Restless Books, 2016.

9 Boots Riley's film *Sorry to Bother You* (Significant Productions, 2018) plays out another possibility of the combinatory: worker's bodies are genetically altered with horse DNA to produce a new and more powerful species of manual laborers.

10 Karl Marx, "Preface (to A Contribution to the Critique of Political Economy)," *Early Writings*, London: Penguin, 1992, 424ff.

11 Marshall Berman, *All That Is Solid Melts into Air: The Experience of Modernity*, New York: Penguin, 1988.

12 McKenzie Wark, *A Hacker Manifesto*, Cambridge, MA: Harvard University Press, 2004.

13 Evegeny Pashukanis, *Law and Marxism*, London: Pluto Press, 1987.

14 James Boyle, *The Public Domain*, New Haven, CT: Yale University Press, 2010.

15 Phillip Kalantzis-Cope, *The Work and Play of the Mind in the Information Age: Whose Property?* London: Palgrave, 2017.

16 Pekka Himanen, *The Hacker Ethic*, New York: Random House, 2002.

17 Matthew Weiner et al. (executive producers), *Mad Men*, Los Angeles: Weiner Bros., 2007–2015.

18 The classic Marxist study of which is Stuart Ewen, *Captains of Consciousness: Advertising and the Social Roots of Commercial Culture*, New York: Basic Books, 2001.

19 Christopher Cantwell and Christopher C. Rogers (creators), *Halt and Catch Fire*, Atlanta, GA: Gran Via Productions and Lockjaw Productions, 2014–2017.

20 I borrowed the term from Paul Virilio, but the concept is closer to the work of Harold Innis, *The Bias of Communication*, Toronto: University of Toronto Press, 2008.

21 Jesse LeCavalier, *The Rule of Logistics: WalMart and the Architecture of Fulfillment*, Minneapolis: University of Minnesota Press, 2016.

22 Leopold Kohr, *The Overdeveloped Nations*, New York: Shocken, 1978.

23 I summed up the debates around this in "From Fordism to Sonyism: Perverse Readings of the New World Order," *New Formations* 16, 1992, 4–54.

24 Karl Marx, *The Revolutions of 1848*, London: Verso, 2010; Karl Marx, *Surveys from Exile*, London: Verso, 2010; Karl Marx, *The First International and After*, London: Verso, 2010.

25 Algirdas Julien Greimas, *On Meaning: Selected Writings in Semiotic Theory*, Minnesota: University of Minneapolis Press, 1987.

26 Anna Tsing, *Friction: An Ethnography of Global Connection*, Princeton, NJ: Princeton University Press, 2005.

27 The Marx Brothers, *Go West* (1940), directed by Edward Buzzell.

28 Michael Hardt and Antonio Negri, *Multitude*, New York: Penguin, 2005. The term has a somewhat different valence in Paolo Virno, *Multitude Between Innovation and Negation*, Los Angeles: Semiotext(e), 2008.

29 Bruce Robbins, *The Beneficiary*, Durham, NC: Duke University Press, 2017.

30 Dave McNary, "Vice Media Employees Unionize," *Variety*, September 21, 2017; Nitasha Tiku, "Why Tech Workers Dissent is Going Viral," *Wired*, June 29, 2018; Daisuke Wakabayashi et at, "Google Walkout: Employees Stage Protest Over Handling of Sexual Harassment," *New York Times*, November 1, 2018. One could connect these recent instances of hacker activisim to more long-standing ones, such as the work of Computer Professionals for Social Responsibility.

31 Popularized by Richard Florida, *The Rise of the Creative Class*, New York: Basic Books, 2014.

32 Franco Berardi, *Soul at Work*, Los Angeles: Semiotext(e), 2009.

33 One could think of cognition in a far wider sense; see Katherine Hayles, *Unthought: The Power of the Cognitive Nonconscious*, Chicago: University of Chicago Press, 2017.

34 Steven Levy, *Hackers*, Sebastopol, CA: O'Reilly Media, 2010. This classic account can be read, in spite of itself, as depicting a moment before hackers in the narrow sense of the term were fully incorporated into a vectoralist mode of production.

35 E. P. Thompson, *William Morris: Romantic to Revolutionary*, Oakland, CA: PM Press, 2011. Morris understood first-hand the contradiction between quality work that produced use value and wage labor that subordinated use value to exchange value.

36 Jack Halberstam, *The Queer Art of Failure*, Durham, NC: Duke University Press, 2010.

37 Francis Fukuyama, *The End of History and the Last Man*, New York: Free Press, 2006.

38 Maurice Dobb, *Theories of Value and Distribution Since Adam Smith*, Cambridge: Cambridge University Press, 1975.

39 Amy Wendling, *Karl Marx on Technology and Alienation*, London: Palgrave, 2009.

40 Tiziana Terranova, *Network Culture: Politics for the Information Age*,

London: Pluto Press, 2004. Labor with the modifier free is still something of a placeholder concept, but has a useful tension in it with the norm of *wage* labor.

41 Marcel Mauss, *The Gift*, Chicago: Hau Books, 2016.

42 Michel Serres, *The Parasite*, Minneapolis: University of Minnesota Press, 2007.

43 Yves Citton, *The Ecology of Attention*, Cambridge, UK: Polity, 2017.

44 I borrowed the term *disintegrating spectacle*, a play on Debord's integrated spectacle, from Jodi Dean, *Blog Theory: Feedback and Capture in the Circuits of Drive*, Cambridge, UK: Polity, 2010.

45 For example: Wendy Brown, *Undoing the Demos: Neoliberalism's Stealth Revolution*, New York: Zone Books, 2015.

46 Randy Martin, *Financialization of Daily Life*, Philadelphia, PA: Temple University Press, 2002.

47 As for example in Antonio Negri, *Marx Beyond Marx: Lessons on the Grundrisse*, New York: Autonomedia, 1992.

48 Melinda Cooper, *Life as Surplus: Biotechnology and Capitalism in the Neoliberal Era*, Seattle: University of Washington Press, 2008.

49 See the introduction to McKenzie Wark, *General Intellects*, New York: Verso, 2017.

50 Randy Martin, *Knowledge LTD: Towards a Social Logic of the Derivative*, Philadelphia, PA: Temple University Press, 2015.

51 Paul B. Préciado, *Testo Junkie*, New York: Feminist Press at CUNY, 2013.

52 Benjamin Bratton, *The Stack: On Software and Sovereignty*, Cambridge, MA: MIT Press, 2016.

53 Amy Wendling, *Karl Marx on Technology and Alienation*, London: Palgrave, 2009.

54 Guy Debord, *in girum imus nocte et consumimur igni*, London: Pelagian Press, 1991, 63.

55 Allan Stoekl, *Bataille's Peak: Energy, Religion and Post-Sustainability*, Minneapolis: University of Minnesota Press, 2007.

3. *The Forces of Production*

1 Wolfgang Schivelbusch, *The Railway Journey: The Industrialization of Time and Space in the Nineteenth Century*, Berkeley: University of California Press, 2014.

2 Anson Rabinbach, *The Human Motor: Energy, Fatigue, and the Origins of Modernity*, Berkeley: University of California Press, 1992.

3 Karl Marx, *Grundrisse*, London: Penguin, 1993, 690ff.

4 David Noble, *The Forces of Production: A Social History of Industrial Automation*, New York: Oxford University Press, 1986.

5 Arthur Rimbaud, *Rimbaud Complete*, trans. Wyatt Mason, New York: The Modern Library, 2002, 366.

6 Maurice Dobb, *Theories of Value and Distribution Since Adam Smith*, Cambridge: Cambridge University Press, 1975.

7 Frederick Beiser, *After Hegel: German Philosophy, 1840–1900*, Princeton, NJ: Princeton University Press, 2014.

8 Amy Wendling, *Karl Marx on Technology and Alienation*, London: Palgrave Macmillan, 2011.

9 Friedrich Engels, *The Dialectics of Nature*, New York: International Publishers, 1940, with an introduction by J. B. S. Haldane.

10 Tristam Hunt, *Marx's General: The Revolutionary Life of Friedrich Engels*, New York: Picador, 2010.

11 Helena Sheehan, *Marxism and the Philosophy of Science*, London: Verso Books, 2017.

12 Loren Graham, *Science, Philosophy, and Human Behavior in the Soviet Union*, New York: Columbia University Press, 1987.

13 Georg Lukács, *Ontology of Social Being* (3 vols.), London: Merlin Press, 1978.

14 Alexander Bogdanov, *The Philosophy of Living Experience*, Chicago: Haymarket, 2017.

15 Gary Werskey, *The Visible College: The Collective Biography of British Scientific Socialists of the 1930s*, New York: Holt, Rinehart & Winston, 1979.

16 J. D. Bernal, *The Social Function of Science*, London: Faber & Faber, 2010.

17 J. D. Bernal, *Science in History* (4 vols.), Cambridge, MA: MIT Press, 1971; V. G. Childe, *Man Makes Himself*, Philadelphia: Coronet Books, 2003; Joseph Needham, *The Grand Titration: Science and Society in East and West*, Toronto: University of Toronto Press, 1979.

18 Donna Haraway, *Modest_Witness@SecondMillennium*, New York: Routledge, 1997.

19 Michel Foucault, "Truth and Power," *Foucault Reader*, New York: Random House, 1984, 66ff.

20 Richard Levins and Richard Lewontin, *The Dialectical Biologist*, Cambridge, MA: Harvard University Press, 1987.

21 Richard Stallman, *Free Software, Free Society: Selected Essays*, Boston: Free Software Foundation, 2002.

22 Asger Jorn, *The Natural Order and Other Texts*, London: Routledge, 2016.

23 Hillary Wainwright, *The Lucas Plan: A New Trades Unionism in the Making?*, New York: Shocken Books, 1981.

24 Antonio Negri, *Marx Beyond Marx*, New York: Autonomedia, 1992.

25 Marx, *Grundrisse*, 706.

26 Georg Lukács, *History and Class Consciousness: Studies in Marxist Dialectics*, trans. R. Livingstone, Cambridge, MA: MIT Press, 1972; Costas Axelos, *Alienation, Praxis and Techne in the Thought of Karl Marx*, trans. R. Bruzina, Austin: University of Texas Press, 1978; Herbert Marcuse, *One Dimensional Man*, Boston: Beacon Press, 1991.

27 Guy Debord, *Society of the Spectacle*, trans. D. Nicholson-Smith, New York: Zone Books, 1995.

28 Andrew Feenberg, *Technosystem: The Social Life of Reason*, Cambridge, MA: Harvard University Press, 2018.

29 Michael Egan, *Barry Commoner and the Science of Survival: The Remaking of American Environmentalism*, Cambridge, MA: MIT Press, 2007.

30 Donna Haraway, *Simians, Cyborgs and Women*, London: Free Associations Books, 1996.

31 I elaborate on the vulgar Marxist reading of Haraway and Barad as an approach to science studies in *Molecular Red*, London: Verso, 2016.

32 Karen Barad, *Meeting the Universe Halfway: Quantum Physics and the Entanglement of Matter and Meaning*, Durham, NC: Duke University Press, 2007.

33 Paul B. Préciado, *Testo Junkie*, New York: The Feminist Press at CUNY, 2013.

34 Paul B. Préciado, "Letter from a Transman to the Old Sexual Regime," *Texte Zur Kunst*, January 22, 2018.

35 For some representative samplings of the ferment of the times, see Jebeesh Bagchi et al., eds., *Sarai Reader*, no. 3, Delhi, 2003; Josephine

Bosma et al., *Readme! ASCII Culture and the Revenge of Knowledge*, New York: Autonomedia, 1999; Annick Buread and Nathalie Magnon, *Connexions: Art, Réseaux, Media*, Paris: École Nationale Superieure des Beaux-Arts, 2002; Maria Fernandez and Faith Wilding, eds., *Domain Errors!: Cyberfeminist Practices*, New York: Autonomedia, 2003.

36 Dmytri Kleiner, *The Telekommunist Manifesto*, Amsterdam: Institute for Network Cultures, 2010.

37 See the work of Michel Bauwens and the P2P Foundation at p2p foundation.net

38 Benjamin Bratton, *The Stack*, Cambridge, MA: MIT Press, 2016.

39 Kleiner, *The Telekommunist Manifesto*, 9.

40 Richard Barbrook with Andy Cameron, *The Internet Revolution*, Amsterdam: Institute for Network Cultures, 2015, 28.

41 "Virtual class" was the coinage of Arthur Kroker and Michael A. Weinstein, *Data-Trash: The Theory of the Virtual Class*, Montreal: New World Perspectives, 1994.

42 Fred Turner, *From Counterculture to Cyberculture*, Chicago: University of Chicago Press, 2008.

43 Angela Davis, ed., *If They Come in the Morning ...*, New York: Verso, 2016.

44 Alvin Toffler, *Future Shock*, New York: Bantam, 1984.

45 Once ascendant, some promotors of the California Ideology became more willing to publicly dispense with democracy as a humanist constraint on the posthuman destiny of technology and its chosen agents. The most interesting trajectory is that of Nick Land, *Fanged Noumena: Collected Writings 1987–2007*, Falmouth: Urbanomic 2011.

46 One might also mention that this yeoman democracy is also built on expropriated land. On the American revolution as imagined from a First Nations perspective, see Wu Ming, *Manituana*, New York: Verso, 2010.

47 Shannon Weinberger, *The Imagineers of War*, New York: Vintage, 2018.

48 Other past examples: Francis Spufford, *Red Plenty*, Minneapolis, MN: Graywolf Press, 2012; Eden Medina, *Cybernetic Revolutionaries*, Cambridge, MA: MIT Press, 2014; Benjamin Peters, *How Not to Network a Nation*, Cambridge, MA: MIT Press, 2017.

4. The Class Location Blues

1 C. Wright Mills, *The Sociological Imagination*, New York: Oxford University Press, 2000; Alvin Gouldner, *For Sociology*, New York: Basic Books, 1974.

2 Stephen Wright, "Digging in the Epistemic Commons," onlineopen.org, March 26, 2007.

3 Anthony Wilden, *System and Structure: Essays in Communication and Exchange*, London: Routledge, 1980.

4 There are actually two books that have the title *Capitalism Without Capital*... As if capital was dead but still had to be treated as eternal, in a negative theology of its absence.

5 Yann Moulier Boutang, *Cognitive Capitalism*, Cambridge, UK: Polity, 2012.

6 Timothy Mitchell, *Carbon Democracy*, New York: Verso, 2013.

7 Erik Olin Wright, *Understanding Class*, London: Verso, 2015.

8 Ibid., 237.

9 Ibid., 236–7.

10 Donald MacKenzie, *An Engine, Not a Camera*, Cambridge, MA: MIT Press, 2008. See also MacKenzie's occasional essays on finance technology and communication for *London Review of Books*, starting in 2008.

11 See McKenzie Wark, *General Intellects*, London: Verso, 2017, 172ff.

12 Wright, *Understanding Class*, 121, 167.

13 Bertold Brecht, *Brecht on Theater*, New York: Hill & Wang, 1971, 91ff.

14 Wright, *Understanding Class*, 17.

15 Fredric Jameson, *The Political Unconscious*, Ithaca, NY: Cornell University Press, 1982, 9.

16 McKenzie Wark, *Gamer Theory*, Cambridge, MA: Harvard University Press, 2007.

17 Wright, *Understanding Class*, 123.

18 Ulrich Beck, "Beyond Class and Nation: Reframing Social Inequalities in a Globalizing World," *British Journal of Sociology* 58: 4, 2007, 679–705.

19 Wright, *Understanding Class*, 154.

20 Kim Weedon and David Grusky, "The Case for a New Class Map," *American Journal of Sociology* 111: 1, 2005, 141–212.

21 Rachel Sherman, *Uneasy Street: The Anxieties of Affluence*, Princeton,

NJ: Princeton University Press, 2017. My New School colleague may object to being called a "Durkheimian," but this is an excellent example of the fine-grained empirical study of class.

22   Wright, *Understanding Class*, 7.

23   Max Weber, *The Protestant Ethic and the Spirit of Capitalism*, London: Penguin, 2002.

24   Wright, *Understanding Class*, 46.

25   Ibid., 31.

26   Silvia Federici, *Caliban and the Witch: Women, the Body and Primitive Accumulation*, New York: Autonomedia, 2004.

27   Wright, *Understanding Class*, 52.

28   Ibid., 53.

29   Ibid., 55.

30   Theodor Adorno and Max Horkheimer, *Dialectic of Enlightenment*, Stanford, CA: Stanford University Press, 2007.

31   Alexander Galloway, *Protocol: How Control Exists after Decentralization*, Cambridge, MA: MIT Press, 2004.

32   Cathy O'Neil, *Weapons of Math Destruction*, New York: Broadway Books, 2017; Virginia Eubanks, *Automating Inequality*, New York: St. Martins Press, 2018; Safiya Umoja Noble, *Algorithms of Oppression*, New York: New York University Press, 2018; Frank Pasquale, *The Black Box Society*, Cambridge, MA: Harvard University Press, 2016.

33   Lucien Goldman, *The Hidden God*, London: Verso, 2016.

34   Jesse McCarthy, "Notes on Trap," *N+1*, no. 32, Fall 2018.

35   Thomas Piketty, *Capital in the Twenty-First Century*, Cambridge, MA: Harvard University Press, 2017.

36   Wright, *Understanding Class*, 133.

37   Ibid., 136.

38   Yochai Benkler, *The Wealth of Networks*, New Haven, CT: Yale University Press, 2007.

39   Matteo Pasquinelli, *Animal Spirits: A Bestiary of the Commons*, Amsterdam: NAi, 2009.

40   David Ricardo, *On the Principles of Political Economy and Taxation*, Cambridge: Cambridge University Press, 1981.

41   Guy Standing, *The Precariat: The New Dangerous Class*, London: Bloomsbury Academic, 2016.

42 In 2018, Alexandria Ocassio-Cortez became a national celebrity by winning a primary against an established Democratic congressman while running on an overtly democratic socialist platform. Her electoral coalition included working class Latinx people but also the more educated (and whiter) people who had more recently moved in to Northern Queens. I live there and did a very modest amount of campaigning for her with the Democratic Socialists of America, who endorsed her in the primary. In its own small way what I saw was the possibility of a worker-hacker alliance, around issues such as rent control, universal health care, socializing the costs of education and a "Green New Deal." Needless to say, this is hardly a radical platform. See Michael Kinnucan, "Why Alexandria Occasio-Cortez Won," *Jacobin*, June 29, 2018.

43 Wolfgang Streeck, "Beneficial Constraints," in J. Rogers Hollingsworth and Robert Boyer, eds., *Contemporary Capitalism*, Cambridge: Cambridge University Press, 1997; Wolfgang Streeck, *How Will Capitalism End?*, London: Verso, 2017, ch. 9.

44 Wright, *Understanding Class*, 183.

45 Ibid., 184.

46 Geoff Dow and Winton Higgins, *Politics Against Pessimism: Social Democratic Possibilities Since Ernst Wigforss*, Bern, Switzerland: Peter Lang, 2013. Winton Higgins was an undergraduate teacher of mine, and so I take the opportunity to thank him here. One might also note that in the Scandinavian countries this tradition of social democracy has come under considerable pressure in more recent times.

47 Trebor Scholz and Nathan Schneider, *Ours to Hack and Own*, New York: O/R Books, 2017.

48 Wright, *Understanding Class*, 143.

49 Benjamin Wallace, "The Twee Party," *New York Magazine*, April 15, 2012.

50 Wright, *Understanding Class*, 239.

51 Ibid., 244.

52 Ibid., 237.

53 John Bellamy Foster, Brett Clark, and Richard York, *The Ecological Rift: Capitalism's War on the Earth*, New York: Monthly Review Press, 2011.

54 Angela McRobbie, *Be Creative*, Cambridge, UK: Polity, 2016.

55 Verso Books, ed., *Where Freedom Starts: Sex Power Violence #MeToo*, New York: Verso Books, 2018.

56 Gerald Raunig, *Dividuum: Machinci Capitalism and Molecular Revolution*, Los Angeles: Semiotext(e), 2016.

57 Franco Berardi, *Soul at Work*, Los Angeles: Semiotext(e), 2009.

58 Cardi B., "Bodak Yellow," 2017. See Robin D. G. Kelley, *Yo' Mama's Disfunktional: Fighting the Culture Wars in Urban America*, Boston: Beacon Press, 1998, which brings Angela Davis's reading of the class politics of blues culture at least up to the nineties.

59 Mark Fisher, *Ghosts of My Life*, Winchester, UK: Zero Books, 2014.

60 Camilla Griggers, *Becoming Woman*, Minneapolis: University of Minnesota Press, 1997; Laurent de Sutter, *Narcocapitalism: Life in the Age of Anaesthesia*, Cambridge, UK: Polity, 2018.

5. A Time Machine Theory of History

1 On the time machine trope, see Fredric Jameson, "In Hyperspace," *London Review of Books* 32: 17, September 2015.

2 Deng Xiaoping, *Fundamental Issues in Present-Day China*, Beijing: Foreign Languages Press, 1987.

3 Masha Gessen, *The Man Without a Face: The Unlikely Rise of Vladimir Putin*, New York: Riverhead Books, 2013.

4 Hannah Arendt, *The Origins of Totalitarianism*, New York: Harcourt, 1973. Arendt is obviously not entirely responsible for the uses this text was put to in Cold War America.

5 See Philip Mirowski and Edward Nik-Khan, *The Knowledge We Have Lost in Information*, New York: Oxford University Press, 2017, for a highly critical account of how orthodox economics handles information.

6 Philip Mirowski, *Machine Dreams: Economics Becomes a Cyborg Science*, Cambridge: Cambridge University Press, 2002.

7 Deng, *Fundamental Issues in Present-Day China*.

8 "Specters of anti-communism" is from Joshua Simon; see Ingo Niermann and Joshua Simon, eds., *Solution 275–294: Communists Anonymous*, Berlin: Sternberg Press, 2017, 19.

9 I owe this idea to Maria Hlavajova and Simon Sheikh, eds., *Former West: Art and the Contemporary after 1989*, Cambridge, MA: MIT Press, 2017, in which this chapter first appeared.

10 On anti-communism as domestic and foreign policy, see Joel Kovel, *Red Hunting in the Promised Land: Anticommunism and the Making of America*, London: Cassell, 1997.

11 Jackie Wang, *Carceral Capitalism*, Los Angeles: Semiotext(e), 2018.

12 Nikita Khrushchev, *Memoirs of Nikita Khrushchev*, University Park: Penn State Press, 2007, 893.

13 *Le grand récit*, which more or less translates as the grand narrative, is from Jean-François Lyotard, *The Postmodern Condition: A Report on Knowledge*, Minneapolis: University of Minnesota Press, 1984.

14 Richard Barbrook, *Imaginary Futures: From Thinking Machines to the Global Village*, London: Pluto Press, 2007.

15 Frank Edward Manuel, *The Prophets of Paris*, New York: Harper, 1965.

16 Robin Mackay and Armen Avanessian, eds., *#Accelerate: The Accelerationist Reader*, Falmouth, UK: Urbanomic, 2014.

17 Rosi Braidotti, *The Posthuman*, Cambridge, UK: Polity, 2013.

18 J. D. Bernal, *The World, the Flesh and the Devil*, Bloomington: Indiana University Press, 1969, 78–80.

19 J. D. Bernal, *The Social Function of Science*, Cambridge, MA: MIT Press, 1969.

20 Andrew Brown, *JD Bernal: The Sage of Science*, Oxford: Oxford University Press, 2007.

21 Kristian Hvidfelt Nielsen, "Enacting the Social Relations of Science," *Public Understanding of Science* 17: 2, 2008, 171–88; Hideto Nakajima, "Kuhn's Structure in Japan," *Social Studies of Science* 42: 3, 2012, 462–6.

22 Radovan Richta et al, *Civilizace na Rozcesti*, Prague: Svoboda, 1966. English translation: Radovan Richta et al, *Civilization at the Crossroads*, Prague: International Arts and Sciences Press, 1969.

23 McKenzie Wark, *A Hacker Manifesto*, Cambridge, MA: Harvard University Press, 2004.

24 Benjamin Peters, *How Not to Network a Nation*, Cambridge, MA: MIT Press, 2016.

25 Robert Buderi, *The Invention That Changed the World*, New York: Simon & Schuster, 1996.

26 See the exchange of views between Bernal and J. B. S. Haldane in *Modern Quarterly* from 1948 to 1949.

27 Georgina Ferry, *Dorothy Hodgkin: A Life*, London: Bloomsbury, 2014.

28 Brenda Maddox, *Rosalind Franklin: The Dark Lady of DNA*, New York: Harper, 2003.

29 Viktor Mayer-Schönberger and Thomas Ramage, *Reinventing Capitalism in the Age of Big Data*, New York: Basic Books, 2018.

30 Francis Spufford, *Red Plenty*, Minneapolis, MN: Greywolf Press, 2012.

31 On Soviet cybernetics, see Slava Gerovitch, *From Newspeak to Cyberspeak*, Cambridge, MA: MIT Press, 2004.

32 See the careful appeals to official Soviet language in Andrei Sakharov, *Progress, Coexistence and Intellectual Freedom*, New York: Norton, 1968.

33 Richard Levins and Richard Lewontin, *The Dialectical Biologist*, Cambridge, MA: Harvard University Press, 1987.

34 Greta Jones, "British Scientists, Lysenko and the Cold War," *Economy & Society* 8: 1, 1978, 26–58.

35 Iris Chang, *Thread of the Silkworm*, New York: Basic Books, 1996.

36 Mary Jo Nye, *Michael Polanyi and His Generation*, Chicago: University of Chicago Press, 2011.

37 Frances Stonor Saunders, *The Cultural Cold War*, New York: The New Press, 2013.

38 Martin Heidegger, *Ponderings II–VI: Black Notebooks 1931–1938*, Bloomington: Indiana University Press, 2016.

39 Hugh Wilford, *The Mighty Wurlitzer: How the CIA Played America*, Cambridge, MA: Harvard University Press, 2009.

40 Henri Saint-Simon, *Social Organization, the Science of Man and Other Writings*, New York: Harper, 1964.

41 Or not. See Mirowski and Nik-Khan, *The Knowledge We Have Lost in Information*, for a highly critical account of how orthodox economics handles information.

42 Chalmers Johnson, *MITI and the Japanese Miracle*, Stanford, CA: Stanford University Press, 1982.

43 John McPhee, "Balloons of War," *The New Yorker*, January 29, 1996.

44 Sylvère Lotringer and Christian Marazzi, eds., *Autonomia: Post-Political Politics*, New York: Semiotext(e), 1980.

45 Paul Ginsborg, *Silvio Berlusconi: Television, Power and Patrimony*, London: Verso, 2005.

46 Nanni Balestrini, *We Want Everything*, London: Verso Books, 2016,

captures the structure of feeling of the revolting southern workers of the time.

47 Sylvère Lotringer and Christian Marazzi, eds., *Autonomia: Post-Political Politics*, New York: Semiotext(e), 1980.

48 Wendy Brown, *Undoing the Demos*, New York: Zone Books, 2015.

49 Marvin Surkin and Dan Georgakas, *Detroit: I Do Mind Dying*, Chicago: Haymarket Books, 2012. Actually many critical labor processes had already moved out of Detroit itself, so by "Detroit" I mean the distributed geography of the car industry rather than the actual city.

50 Clearly a topic in need of far more sensitive handling than I can give it here. See Federico Finchelstein, *From Fascism to Populism in History*, Berkeley: University of California Press, 2017.

51 Angela Y. Davis, *Are Prisons Obsolete?* New York: Seven Stories Press, 2003.

52 Sharon Weinberger, *The Imagineers of War: The Untold Story of DARPA*, New York: Knopf, 2017.

53 Benjamin Bratton, *The Stack: On Software and Sovereignty*, Cambridge, MA: MIT Press, 2016.

54 David Halberstam, *The Reckoning*, New York: William Morrow, 1986.

55 Tiziana Terranova, *Network Cultures: Politics for the Information Age*, London: Pluto Press, 2004.

56 Sandra Braman, *Change of State: Information, Policy, Power*, Cambridge, MA: MIT Press, 2009.

57 Guy Debord, *Comments on the Society of the Spectacle*, New York: Verso, 2011.

58 On the post-Soviet period, see Tony Wood, *Russia Without Putin: Money, Power and the Myths of the New Cold War*, New York: Verso, 2018.

59 Deng, *Fundamental Issues on Present-Day China*.

60 Arif Dirlick, *Complicities: The People's Republic of China in Global Capitalism*, Chicago: Prickly Paradigm, 2017.

61 Xi Jinping, "Report to the 19th CPC National Congress," *China Daily*, October 18, 2017.

62 McKenzie Wark, *Virtual Geography*, Bloomington: Indiana University Press, 1994.

63 Bratton, *The Stack*.

64 Adrian Chan, *Chinese Marxism*, London: Continuum, 2003.

65 Laikwang Pang, *The Art of Cloning: Creative Production During China's Cultural Revolution*, London: Verso, 2017.

66 Yuk Hui, *The Question Concerning Technology in China*, Falmouth, UK: Urbanomic, 2016, 190–97. This brilliant book notes in passing that Deng drew in part on Engels-inspired Marxist theories of technology to pose questions about industrial efficiency in order to develop a policy for the rapid expansion of the forces of production.

67 Xi Jinping, *The Governance of China*, vol. 2, Shanghai: Shanghai Press, 2018.

68 Daniel Vukovich, *Illiberal China*, Singapore: Palgrave Macmillan, 2019, ably poses the problem of seeing like a *different* state (a problem that I obviously cannot do justice to in these speculative remarks).

69 Jan Zalasiewicz, Colin N. Waters, Mark Williams, and Colin Peter Summerhayes, eds., *The Anthropocene as a Geological Time Unit: A Guide to the Scientific Evidence and Current Debate*, Cambridge: Cambridge University Press, 2019.

6. *Nature as Extrapolation and Inertia*

1 Sianne Ngai, *Ugly Feelings*, Cambridge, MA: Harvard University Press, 2007.

2 Peter L. Berger and Thomas Luckman, *The Social Construction of Reality*, New York: Anchor, 1967. This is one way of thinking the direction in which science studies moved on from the sociology of knowledge.

3 Jason W. Moore, *Capitalism in the Web of Life*, New York: Verso, 2015.

4 Paul Burkett, *Marx and Nature*, Chicago: Haymarket Books, 2014.

5 E. P. Thompson, *Exterminism and the Cold War*, London: Verso, 1987. See also John Carl Baker, "Notes on Late Exterminism," published on the Verso blog, June 16, 2017.

6 Robert J. C. Young, *White Mythologies*, New York: Routledge, 2004. Young offers a strong critique of the Sartrean project outlined in this essay, from a postcolonial perspective.

7 Vivek Chibber, *Postcolonial Theory and the Specter of Capital*, London: Verso, 2013.

8 Gilles Deleuze and Félix Guattari, *Anti-Oedipus*, London: Penguin,

2009; Jean-François Lyotard, *Libidinal Economy*, London: Bloomsbury Academic, 2015; Benjamin Noys, *Malign Velocities*, Winchester, UK: Zero Books, 2014.

9   Nick Land, *Fanged Noumena*, Falmouth, UK: Urbanomic, 2013; McKenzie Wark, *A Hacker Manifesto*, Cambridge, MA: Harvard University Press, 2004.

10 Wark, *A Hacker Manifesto*, a détournement combining passages from: 1, 33, 20, 270.

11 Ibid., combining passages from: 327, 98.

12 Ibid, 246. The quotation from Gilles Deleuze is from, *Negations*, New York: University of Columbia Press, 1995, 127.

13 Nick Srnicek and Alex Williams, *Inventing the Future: Postcapitalism and a World Without Work*, London: Verso Books, 2016.

14 On Bernal's influence on Wilson, see Andrew Brown, *J. D. Bernal: The Sage of Science*, Oxford: Oxford University Press, 2006, 437ff.

15 Harold Wilson, in *Labour Party Annual Conference Report*, 1963, 139–40.

16 Kathi Weeks, *The Problem with Work*, Durham, NC: Duke University Press, 2011.

17 McKenzie Wark, *Gamer Theory*, Cambridge, MA: Harvard University Press, 2007.

18 Jason W. Moore, ed., *Anthropocene or Capitalocene? Nature, History, and the Crisis of Capitalism*, Oakland, CA: PM Press, 2016.

19 Donna Haraway, *Manifestly Haraway*, Minneapolis: University of Minnesota Press, 2016.

20 Joseph Needham, *Time: The Refreshing River*, London: Allen & Unwin, 1943, 20.

21 Ernst Mach, *The Analysis of Sensations*, Mineola, NY: Dover, 2015.

22 N. I. Bukharin et al., *Science at the Cross Roads: Papers from The Second International Congress of the History of Science and Technology 1931*, London: Routledge, 2014.

23 Needham, *Time*, 75ff.

24 Joseph Needham, *Biochemistry and Morphogenesis*, Cambridge: Cambridge University Press, 1942.

25 Needham's reading of Lucretius put the stress on the bonds rather than the particles. See Thomas Nail, *Lucretius I: An Ontology of Motion*, Edinburgh, Scotland: Edinburgh University Press, 2018. On Marx

and Lucretius, see John Bellamy Foster, *Marx's Ecology*, New York: Monthly Review Press, 2000.

26 Donna Haraway, *Crystals, Fabrics and Fields*, Berkeley, CA: North Atlantic Books, 2004, 101ff.

27 Joseph Needham, *Science and Civilization in China*, Vol. 1, Cambridge: Cambridge University Press, 1954.

28 Yuk Hui, *The Question Concerning Technology in China*, Falmouth, UK: Urbanomic, 2016.

29 Jean-Paul Sartre, *Being and Nothingness*, New York: Washington Square Press, 1993.

30 Norman Geras, *Marx and Human Nature: Refutation of a Legend*, London: Verso, 2016.

31 One can see here the beginnings of François Laruelle, *Introduction to Non-Marxism*, Minneapolis, MN: Univocal, 2015.

32 One can see how this ends up in Derrida as the theme of deferral.

33 Jean-Paul Sartre, *Nausea*, New York: New Directions, 2013.

34 Martin Jay, *Marxism and Totality: The Adventures of a Concept from Lukács to Habermas*, Berkeley: University of California Press, 1987, 341. This whole chapter is heavily indebted to Jay and to Fredric Jameson's commentaries on the *Critique of Dialectical Reason*.

35 Sartre, *Being and Nothingness*, 754.

36 Jean-Paul Sartre, *What Is Literature?* London: Routledge, 2001.

37 See "The Flies" in Jean-Paul Sartre, *No Exit and Three Other Plays*, New York: Vintage, 1987.

38 Guy Debord, "Report on the Construction of Situations," in Tom McDonough, ed., *Guy Debord and the Situationist International*, Cambridge, MA: MIT Press, 2004.

39 Slavoj Žižek, *In Defense of Lost Causes*, London: Verso, 2017, 175ff.

40 Maurice Merleau-Ponty, *Adventures of the Dialectic*, Evanston, IL: Northwestern University Press, 1973, 64, emphasis added.

41 On which see McKenzie Wark, *Molecular Red*, New York: Verso, 2016.

42 Merleau-Ponty, *Adventures of the Dialectic*, 90.

43 Martin Heidegger, "Letter on Humanism," *Basic Writings*, New York: Harper, 2008.

44 Jean-Paul Sartre, *Critique of Dialectical Reason*, London: Verso, 2004. I am much indebted to Jameson's introduction.

45 Henri Lefebvre, *Critique of Everyday Life, Vol. 2*, London: Verso, 2008.

46 Alain Badiou, *Being and Event*, London: Bloomsbury Academic, 2013.

47 A détournement of Marx: "Men make their own history, but they do not make it as they please ..." from "The Eighteen Brumaire of Napoleon Bonaparte," *Surveys from Exile*, London: Verso, 2010.

48 Karl Marx and Friedrich Engels, *The Communist Manifesto: A Modern Edition*, London: Verso, 2012, 38.

49 Sartre, *Critique of Dialectical Reason*, 260.

50 Alfie Bown and Dan Bristow, *Post-Memes: Seizing the Memes of Production*, Goleta, CA: Punctum Books, 2019.

51 Further elaborated by Félix Guattari, *Three Ecologies*, London: Bloomsbury Academic, 2014.

52 Writers for the 99%, *Occupying Wall Street: The Inside Story of an Action than Changed America*, Chicago: Haymarket, 2012.

53 Sheila Fitzpatrick, *Tear Off the Masks! Identity and Imposture in Twentieth Century Russia*, Princeton, NJ: Princeton University Press, 2005.

54 Jean-Paul Sartre, *Search for a Method*, New York: Vintage, 1968, 51.

55 See Ray Brassier, *Nihil Unbound: Enlightenment and Extinction*, London: Palgrave, 2007, and also his unpublished essay "On Prometheanism (and its critics)," 2013.

56 Karen Barad, *Meeting the Universe Halfway: Quantum Physics and the Entanglement of Matter and Meaning*, Durham, NC: Duke University Press, 2007.

57 The Situationist International détourned the concept of situation from Sartre, but made its indeterminacy the key to a practice. See McKenzie Wark, *The Beach Beneath the Street*, London: Verso, 2011.

58 On Marx and Malthus, see John Bellamy Foster, *Marx's Ecology*, New York: Monthly Review Press, 2000.

59 Drew Milne, "Lichen for Marxists," quote from *In Darkest Capital: The Collected Poems*, Manchester, England: Carcanet, 2017, 376.

60 Francis Ponge, *Mute Objects of Expression*, New York: Archipelago Books, 2008.

61 Drew Milne, "The Makings of the Biotariat," unpublished, quoted with permission.

62 Antonin Artaud, *Watchfiends and Rack Screams: Works from the Final Period*, Boston: Exact Change Press, 2004.

63 Richard Crossman, ed., *The God That Failed*, New York: Columbia University Press, 2001.

7. *Four Cheers for Vulgarity!!!!*

1 Georges Bataille, *Visions of Excess: Selected Writings 1927–1939*, Minneapolis: University of Minnesota Press, 1984; Aimé Césaire, Discourse on Colonialism, New York: Monthly Review Press, 2001; Raymond Williams, *Resources of Hope: Culture, Democracy Socialism*, London: Verso Books, 2016. Silvia Federici, *Caliban and the Witch: Women, the Body and Primitive Accumulation*, New York: Autonomedia, 2004.

2 Guy Debord, *Panegyric*, London: Verso, 2009; Paul B. Préciado, *Testo Junkie*, New York: Feminist Press, 2013.

3 Perry Anderson, *Considerations on Western Marxism*, London: Verso, 1976.

4 Georg Lukács, "What is Orthodox Marxism?" *History and Class Consciousness*, London: Merlin Press, 1971.

5 Walter Benjamin, "On the Concept of History" (1940), trans. Dennis Redmond, http://www.marxists.org

6 Joseph Dietzgen, *The Nature of Human Brain-Work: An Introduction to Dialectics*, Oakland, CA: PM Press, 2010.

7 Theodor Adorno, *Minima Moralia*, London: Verso, 2006, 43–4.

8 Maurice Merleau-Ponty, *The Phenomenology of Perception*, London: Routledge Kegan Paul, 1962, 171–2.

9 Louis Althusser, *Reading* Capital, trans. Ben Brewster, London: New Left Books, 1970, http://www.marxists.org

10 E. P. Thompson, *The Poverty of Theory*, New York: Monthly Review Press, 1978; Perry Anderson, *Arguments Within English Marxism*, London: Verso, 1980.

11 E. P. Thompson, "Caudwell," *Socialist Register*, 1977, 228–76, https://www.marxists.org. See Christopher Caudwell, *Studies and Further Studies in a Dying Culture*, New York: Monthly Review Press, 1971, for the once best-known work of this underappreciated vulgar Marxist.

12 https://books.google.com/ngrams.

13 Antonio Negri, *Marx Beyond Marx*, New York: Autonomedia, 1992, 137.

14 Kojin Karatani, *Transcritique*, Cambridge MA: MIT Press, 2005, 10;

Ernesto Laclau, *Emancipations*, London: Verso Books, 2005, 87; Cornell West, *The Cornel West Reader*, New York: Perseus Books, 1999, 9, 72, 260.

15 Fredric Jameson, *Postmodernism, or, The Cultural Logic of Late Capitalism*, London: Verso Books, 2012, 297; Terry Eagleton, *Marxism and Literary Criticism*, Berkeley, CA: University of California Press, 1976, passim; Terry Eagleton, *Ideology: An Introduction*, London: Verso Books, 2007, 100; Julia Kristeva, *Desire in Language*, New York: Columbia University Press, 1982, 16; Samir Amin, *Imperialism and Unequal Development*, New York: Monthly Review Press, 1979, 236.

16 Jean Baudrillard, *Mirror of Production*, Candor, NY: Telos Press, 1975, 37.

17 Gayle Rubin, *Deviations*, Durham, NC: Duke University Press, 2011, 292.

18 Laura Mulvey, *Fetishism and Curiosity*, Bloomington: Indiana University Press, 1996, xiii.

19 John Bellamy Foster, *Marx's Ecology*, New York: Monthly Review Press, 2000.

20 Slavoj Žižek, *Žižek's Jokes*, Cambridge, MA: MIT Press, 2016.

21 McKenzie Wark, *Molecular Red*, London: Verso, 2016.

22 Andrei Platonov, *Chevengur*, Ann Arbor, MI: Ardis, 1978.

23 Comrades face the same dangers: Ibid., 141.

24 Living on secondary ideas: Ibid., 283.

25 Angela Davis, *An Autobiography*, New York: International Publishers, 1988, 192.

26 Angela Y. Davis, *Blues Legacies and Black Feminism*, New York: Vintage, 1999.

27 Ibid., 141.

28 Karl Marx, "Contribution to the Critique of Hegel's Philosophy of Right," *Early Writings*, Harmondsworth: Penguin / New Left Books, 1975, 244.

29 Davis, *Blues Legacies and Black Feminism*, 120.

30 Herbart Marcuse, *The Aesthetic Dimension*, Boston: Beacon Press, 1975. Interestingly, Marcuse does not use the expression *vulgar Marxism* often. See for example Douglas Kellner, ed., *The New Left and the Sixties: The*

Collected Papers of Herbert Marcuse, London: Routledge, 2005, 140. But he used *vulgar* as a modifier quite a lot.

31 Siva Vaidhayanathan, *Copyrights and Copywrongs*, New York: New York University Press, 2003.

32 Angela Y. Davis, *The Meaning of Freedom and Other Difficult Dialogues*, San Francisco, CA: City Lights Books, 2012.

33 Pier Paolo Pasolini, *The Street Kids*, New York: Europa Editions, 2016.

34 Pier Paolo Pasolini, *Heretical Empiricism*, Washington, DC: New Academia, 2005.

35 For all their differences, Debord and Pasolini shared a blind hatred of the outward or Durkheimian symptoms of a rising hacker class, even though they belonged to it, and were as a consequence blinded as to its actual productive role. See Guy Debord, *Complete Cinematic Works*, Chico, CA: AK Press, 2005, in particular the magnificent script for *in girum imus nocte et consumimur igni*.

36 Maurizio Lazzarato, *Signs and Machines: Capitalism and the Production of Subjectivity*, Los Angeles: Semiotext(e), 2014.

37 See McKenzie Wark, "The Avant-Garde Never Gives Up," *Lana Turner*, no. 7, 2014, on Pasolini's avant-garde nemesis, Edoardo Sanguineti.

38 Asger Jorn, *The Natural Order and Other Texts*, Farnham, UK: Ashgate, 2002, 135.

39 C. Wright Mills, *The Power Elite*, Oxford: Oxford University Press, 1957.

40 See McKenzie Wark, *The Beach Beneath the Street*, London: Verso, 2015, Chapter 4.

41 On gender in media production, see Friedrich Kittler, *Discourse Networks*, Stanford, CA: Stanford University Press, 1992; Friedrich Kittler, *Gramophone, Film, Typewriter*, Stanford, CA: Stanford University Press, 1999.

42 Paolo Virno, *Deja Vu and the End of History*, London: Verso, 2015.

43 The over-enthusiasm of the four cheers is a reversal of E. M. Forster, *Two Cheers for Democracy*, New York: Mariner Books, 1962.

44 Compare these texts: Sigfried Giedion, *Mechanization Takes Command*, Minneapolis: University of Minnesota Press, 2014, and Lev Manovich, *Software Takes Command*, London: Bloomsbury, 2013.

Conclusion: A Night at the Movies

1 Raoul Peck (director), *The Young Karl Marx*, Paris: Diaphana Films, 2017.

2 For a more sophisticated appreciation of realism, see T. J. Clark, *Image of the People: Gustave Courbert and the 1848 Revolution*, Berkeley: University of California Press, 1999.

3 Friedrich Engels, *The Condition of the Working Class in England*, Oxford World's Classics, Oxford: Oxford University Press, 2009; Andrew Merrifield, *Metromarxism: A Marxist Tale of the City*, London: Routledge, 2002.